GOING NOWHERE:

EXPLORING LONDON'S ABANDONED PLACES

Text by Nick Freeth
Photography by Olivia Landsberg

BAFFIN BOOKS UK

GOING NOWHERE: EXPLORING LONDON'S ABANDONED PLACES
Text by Nick Freeth
Photography by Olivia Landsberg

Cover designed by Sue Pressley

The Authors assert their right to be identified in relation to the Work on the title page in
the following form:
NICK FREETH and OLIVIA LANDSBERG

Text © Nick Freeth 2017
Photographs © Olivia Landsberg 2017

Published by Baffin Books UK, London
www.baffinbooks.simplesite.com

ISBN: 978-1-9998198-2-8

CONTENTS

Acknowledgements	5
Setting the scene: tuned to London?	6
INNER ZONE:	
Bishopsgate's brick spine	14
The City's unbuilt rail route	26
Goodman's Fields Viaduct and 'the Tilbury'	32
121 Westminster Bridge Road: 'The Sally Port to Eternity'	38
MIDDLE ZONE:	
The Limehouse Curve	46
Pedestrians in the Rotherhithe Tunnel	54
Millwall: 'Desolation-Land'	66
A view from the EGGS Bridge	72
Beside the tracks in Hammersmith and East Putney	80
OUTER ZONE:	
An interlude at Mill Hill East	88
M12 – the motorway that never was	96
The Crescent Wood Tunnel	104
Croydon Airport	112
The line to Chessington	120
Deptford to 'the jaws of the ocean' and Red Sands	126
POSTSCRIPT	141
Notes	143
About the authors	151

ACKNOWLEDGEMENTS

Special thanks to:
Catriona Duncan, Assistant Property Manager at the Broadgate Tower;
Jenni Boswell-Jones and Ismail Saray (ArtZone) and John Archer (London Borough of Tower Hamlets) for arranging our visit to the Goodman's Fields Viaduct;
Bernadette McNicholas of the Canal River Trust and Sheamus Tierney (Project Manager for Ardmore at Limehouse) for enabling us to visit Limehouse's Accumulator Tower;
David Marriot Cooper and everyone at Project Redsand;
Pam Cooper (X-Pilot Bookings), and the crew of the *X-Pilot*.

The British Library;
The National Archives at Kew;
The old-maps.co.uk historical map archive;
The Newham Archives and Local Studies Library.

The quotation on p.48 comes from www.imvisitinglondon.com/limehousebasin.html – thanks to Hugo Marchant for permission to use it.

Some of the quoted stories from older newspapers appeared simultaneously in several different publications around the UK. I've sought to trace and credit the original sources for these items (rather than giving a reference to one of the papers that reprinted them), but haven't always been successful.

While working on this book, we've been careful not to trespass, and would urge readers visiting the sites we've featured to abide by all applicable laws, regulations and restrictions, and to stay safe.

London stretches outwards: the view southeast from The Shard

SETTING THE SCENE: TUNED TO LONDON?

If London were lost, or suspected of a crime, its 'wanted' poster would probably display one of its tourist attractions: Tower Bridge, Nelson's Column, the dome of St. Paul's, or the Palace of Westminster. But the city's range of identities is too diverse and bewildering to be summed up by any single structure, however iconic. Even a mug book of its most celebrated sights would mislead seekers and witnesses – who, as they flicked through the pages, might fail to notice the real place slipping away from them, clad in a different shape.

And it's undeniably the case that London's architectural set-pieces are sometimes given short shrift by its residents. We get tired of the postcards, table mats, teacloths and sauce bottles bearing their likenesses, and scarcely give the buildings themselves a second glance as we go about our business, though we may doff our hats to them in grudging recognition of their heavyweight greatness. After all, the capital they represent is a focus for power, commerce and finance; a destination to which the trains have always gone 'up'; and a place that's often been portrayed as a 'promised land' - though its particular brand of promise differs from the good fortune you might hope for at Monte Carlo (where the man in the song famously broke the bank), or in the Big Rock Candy Mountain, with its cigarette trees, soda-water fountain and singing bluebird. London doesn't readily give up its treasures, as the apparently naïve Irishman in Percy French's *Mountains of Mourne* discovers while watching and then joining its labourers:

> They don't sow potatoes nor barley nor wheat
> But there's gangs of them diggin' for gold in the street.
> At least, when I asked them that's what I was told
> So I just took a hand at this diggin' for gold;
> But for all that I've found there, I might as well be
> Where the Mountains of Mourne sweep down to the sea.

Even London's mellifluous bells have a peremptory edge. Their oranges and lemons mingle with demands for money...

> You owe me five farthings...
> When will you pay me?...
> When I grow rich...
> When will that be?

...and the mythical peals that summoned Dick Whittington back from Holloway are a commanding, not especially friendly augury of a grand title, short (at least in the three-line version of the 'Turn again' nursery rhyme that I know best) on specific promises of good fellowship.

> Turn again, Whittington,
> Thou worthy citizen,
> Lord Mayor of London!

The real Sir Richard Whittington's Lord Mayoralty began in 1397, and London's material significance grew steadily over subsequent centuries. It attained an equally imposing symbolic status, and was compared to and even conflated with the biblical New Jerusalem. Some of these allusions and parallels may be mere literary conceits, but others are words from the Scriptures that take on a special significance in a 'local' context - like Psalm 122, which has a clear subtext when heard at British coronations in the richness of Sir Hubert Parry's choral setting.

> I was glad when they said unto me: We will go into the house of the Lord.
> Our feet shall stand in thy gates: O Jerusalem.
> Jerusalem is builded as a city: that is at unity in itself...
> O pray for the peace of Jerusalem: they shall prosper that love thee.
> Peace be within thy walls: and plenteousness within thy palaces.

Here, "the house of the Lord" is Westminster Abbey, "Jerusalem" is London, and, by extension, "England's green and pleasant land" (recalling another, even more famous composition of Parry's); while the "city" - to which, in a different verse from the same psalm, "the tribes go up", just like the trains - possesses a mystical unity impossible to square with reality.

These metaphors are heady ones, and I'm probably not the first Londoner to find them colouring my perception of other words and music. Even the lovely old American spiritual, *Twelve Gates to the City*, acquires a local spin in my mind: I associate its lyrics with the London I'm familiar with...

> Oh, what a beautiful city,
> Twelve gates to the city, Hallelu...
> Well, there's three gates in the east, three gates in the west,
> Three gates in the north, three gates in the south,
> That makes twelve gates to the city, Hallelu...

...though I know it only ever had *seven* main gates, and that arbitrarily adding a few more (Forest Gate in the east? New Cross Gate in the south?) will do nothing to make sense of my daft take on the song.

Such reveries sit awkwardly alongside the London we inhabit. The real metropolis lacks the ordered symmetry ascribed to New Jerusalem. Instead, it's a place whose seeping, oozing growth was being described, as long ago as 1890 (in Sir Arthur Conan Doyle's classic Sherlock Holmes story, *The Sign of Four*) as "monster tentacles which the giant city was throwing out into the country." The notion of London as a gelatinous, swelling and spreading organism is a vivid one; and the animal analogy stays in my mind when I consider the bruised, scarred areas that are a by-product of the city's constant changes and adaptions. The most striking of them are the remnants of its abandoned viaducts, tunnels, concrete strips and jetties: semi-forgotten fabrications that once served its trains, boats and planes, but are now surplus to its requirements. These alternative landmarks have curious, stuttering stories to tell - tales that contrast sharply with the polished, haughty narratives of the heritage sites – and this book will be focusing on their upheavals, transformations and significance.

***

I like to walk around the capital. Examining it slowly on foot, instead of being whisked about on public transport, is revealing, but frustrating. In the midst of people and traffic, or standing in the shadow of a tall tower, I struggle to obtain a clear perspective on my surroundings, and find myself getting nostalgic for the autocratic reassurance of the old BBC World Service station ID, barked out through the stiff upper lips of its continuity announcers: "You're tuned to London." Do I sometimes drift 'out of tune' with the place? If so, my perambulations could be a semi-conscious attempt to improve my reception with the psychic equivalent of an outstretched short-wave aerial. Analogue radio signals, as dedicated listeners know, are subject to interference, but can be picked up in improbable locations and fringe areas. For me, these unexpected clear spots include London's edges, to which I'm attracted because they sometimes allow me to see its roads and buildings in a single looming or receding mass, and because I can try to detect a definable change (a sense of loss or alteration, or at least a twitch on my signal meter) when I step outside them.

But this approach isn't always successful. No transformation occurs at, say, the neatly signposted, visually insignificant London/Essex county line near Roding Valley station on the Central Line; and elsewhere, my attempts to pinpoint where the last ribbons of houses peter out, and streets finally give way to fields, are seldom conclusive. Our sprawling metropolis has no walls: its perimeter is elastic, straining against what Iain Sinclair calls the "security collar" of the M25, but sometimes loose enough to allow patches of farmland and countryside to flourish inside. There are no longer any real "gates to the city", either: just bridges, tunnels and exits to make coming and going easy for cars and lorries – unless they and their occupants are unlucky enough to get stuck in a jam, pulled over by police (Met officers are more mobile and energetic than the Big Rock Candy Mountain's wooden-legged cops), or immobilised with a tyre shredder.

And close to the highways and train tracks linking London to the rest of the country are its other inputs and outputs: power lines, phone cables, physically and wirelessly connected utilities. A buzzing sense of flow - of human, electrical, electronic and vehicular traffic in perpetual motion, 24/7 – infects much of the capital's threshold. It has a bleeding gum-line, often swollen and disfigured by slip roads, verges and signposts; pierced by headlights and street lamps cutting through what would otherwise be semi-rural darkness; and agitated, even deranged, by the restlessness surrounding it.

Retreating from this turmoil, I'm repeatedly drawn back to the now-disconnected stubs of London's transport infrastructure that I mentioned earlier: what I think of as its 'going nowhere' places. Some, such as the disused viaducts and bridges, are literally high and dry, their crumbling obsolescence ignored and disdained by the lively, purposeful areas around them. Others are less prominent, though still easily visible; but they all represent breaks and weakenings in the capital's 'jelly', obstacles to its surging traffic and energy. And they exist in close proximity to daily life; it takes no more than a few steps to move into or out of them. Perhaps their physical remains, and the atmospheres and echoes of the past they preserve, can give me the sense of London I fail to find elsewhere: maybe clarify my idea of what the city is by showing me what it seems to have withdrawn from, and what's been uncovered or risen to the surface in the process?

I'm content simply to describe such sites as 'strange', and don't seek to give them the kind of magical significance accorded to standing stones or burial mounds. There are usually straightforward economic or practical reasons why they've fallen off the grid. But you don't have to be an occultist or a psychogeographer to react more intuitively to them. Seen at a distance, or from an elevated vantage point, the more massive ruins stand out in sharp relief to their surroundings. The forgivingly inclusive fabric of London can knit together many kinds of landmarks, old and new: to my eyes, the Gherkin and the Onion, if not yet the Walkie-Talkie, exist quite harmoniously alongside more traditional buildings. (Don't such cosy nicknames suggest that we're already on the way to accepting these initially controversial edifices?) But - to choose an obvious example - the Braithwaite viaduct that once served the Bishopsgate goods yard seems incapable of being assimilated or digested; it decays and sprouts grass and weeds, but will never fall back into its surroundings unless it's blown up – or, perhaps, subjected to the "limited demolition and structural intervention" euphemistically proposed by developers. So there it stands, its derelict brickwork like damaged, left-behind fragments of a spine; a forsaken ridge whose discordance, and that of the more obscure 'leftovers' we'll be exploring elsewhere, is both unsettling and mysteriously compelling.

These spots are mostly open to some degree of public access, though we've had a few obstacles to surmount, permissions to obtain and ladders to climb while gathering material for this book. Nearly all our requests were granted with great kindness, although one more grudging but still good-natured response sticks in my mind: "You're taking pictures here already, so you might as well go on doing it…"

Our chosen sites are presented in three 'zones':
- a central area whose 'going nowhere' locations are all railway-related;
- a second geographical band, a little farther out, that takes in a disused pedestrian route, as well as a truncated road bridge;
- and a third, suburban zone, including a fragment of a never-built motorway, and a former airport.

Our attention finally shifts to the Thames, as we explore the Deptford foreshore, then head out into 'the jaws of the ocean' for a visit to Red Sands, one of the now abandoned anti-aircraft Army Forts built during World War II by Guy Maunsell.

Having - sometimes literally - stumbled across many of these places on my wanderings, I've been eager to learn more about them, and to quote, in this book, from the people who knew and used them. I hope their words, often garnered from old newspapers and magazines, will have the effect of re-populating and re-vivifying what is now empty and silent; they're presented alongside factual details gleaned from my research in libraries, archives and online. Mingled with these realities are my own more subjective reactions to each location.

The Essex boundary near Roding Valley station

"The city's gum-line, swollen and disfigured by verges and signposts…"

Tall towers; looming or receding streets

The Braithwaite Viaduct, the main line tracks serving Liverpool Street, and (on the left) Shoreditch High Street Overground station, seen from the top of Broadgate Tower

INNER ZONE

BISHOPSGATE'S BRICK SPINE

London's Liverpool Street station has eighteen platforms, serving six tracks. Anyone travelling in or out is swallowed or disgorged by its 'throat' - the place beyond the platforms where the lines divide or combine.

Expulsion from here, as the train gathers speed at the start of a journey, can be disorientating for eastbound ('down') passengers. After the station's artificial light, there are murky tunnels, with glimpses upwards and sideways through fissures and cavities. Some of the tracks then emerge into a deep, still gloomy cutting: there aren't many visual clues to its location, but a few straggles of plants can be seen. Seconds later, the train is in the open, and as it gathers speed, a succession of more recognisable sights fly past the carriage windows.

It's easier to examine the cutting from the road, though a little peering over walls and through grilles is required. It runs in a chasm beside Quaker Street in Shoreditch, and above it is a massive, overgrown viaduct designed by a Victorian engineer, John Braithwaite, for whom part of nearby Wheler Street has recently been renamed. Built to serve the Eastern Counties Railway's Shoreditch terminus, which opened in July 1840, it was originally about a mile and a quarter long; the 850 feet of it that survives formed part of the goods depot that replaced the station. The viaduct was in use until the 1960s, and has now achieved Grade II listing as "a building of special interest, warranting every effort to preserve it."

The railway, past and present, is so inescapable around here that it's hard to get a sense of how the area was before its arrival, though maps, documents, and local street names provide a few hints. Quaker Street was formerly Westbury Street, named for Sir William Wheler of Westbury, the seventeenth-century MP and landowner who developed the area. There was once a Friends Meeting House on its corner, and among the many Quakers arrested for preaching in the locality was William Penn, founder of America's Pennsylvania Colony ('The Quaker Province'). Shoreditch station offered its passengers a more limited range of destinations: initially, they could go no further than Brentwood in Essex.

The route into Shoreditch, with its "roadway [i.e. tracks]...at an elevation of upwards of twenty feet above the level of the street",[1] was costly and difficult to construct, due to the "crowded building property, intersected with sewers, old ditches and numerous cesspools"[2] that lay in its path. The Eastern Counties Railway imposed itself as ruthlessly upon its neighbours as on its surroundings. As early as November 1840, residents and tradesmen were complaining about the company's proposed erection of a "thick wall", claiming that it would "render impassable for carts a street called Goddard's-rents, besides blocking up or obstructing the lights of existing houses...One of the inhabitants was an innkeeper [who] could get no beer into his cellar, another a baker [who] could get no flour to make his bread; a third a carman with ten or twelve children, whose sole subsistence arose from his cart, that he could no longer use, were this application granted."[3] The ECR directors' assertion that the road to be blocked off was "useless" brought a scornful rejoinder from the parliamentary agent representing the residents:

"How could a road be deemed useless which was...so absolutely necessary for the existing inhabitants? True, the Railway Directors might desire to make it useless, in order to make the buildings worthless, and so obtain them for a small proportion of their present value. This was no improbable supposition..."[4]

The Shoreditch terminus, renamed Bishopsgate in 1846, was steadily outgrown by the railway, whose services reached Ipswich that year, and later extended as far as Norwich. In 1874, passengers on what was now the Great Eastern began using a new station at Liverpool Street. Once it opened fully, Bishopsgate was largely demolished, and replaced by a massive goods yard, inaugurated in 1881: a contemporary press report described it as occupying "the old station's site and a vast deal of space besides."[5] It had a three-storey covered area, topped with an iron and glass roof, and incorporated railway tracks running on Braithwaite's viaduct. There were facilities for road vehicles, a warehouse, and offices for the GER clerks, while an "open part lying beyond [measured] about 900 feet by 400 feet."[6]

Bishopsgate's principal traffic was fish, farm produce from East Anglia, and cargo from the port of Harwich; during the 1930s, as many as 850 wagons were passing through it every day. A decline in rail freight reduced the depot's post-war viability, but its fate was sealed by a more immediate and devastating event: the fire that broke out there on the morning of Saturday 5th December 1964. Walls and floors cracked and collapsed as winds whipped up the blaze. Some of the materials stored on the premises exploded, two customs officers lost their lives, and £5 million of damage was caused, putting an end to the working life of the yard. It lay derelict for years, and began to be bulldozed in 2003, prior to the construction of the new Shoreditch High Street Overground station. Sports pitches now occupy some of the site, and the entire area is the subject of controversial development plans, though assurances have been given that the viaduct itself will be "celebrated" and "re-used" as an essential part of them.

***

When I lived in Whitechapel during the 1980s and 90s, my route to work took me along the boundary of the Bishopsgate yard. I scarcely gave it a glance, and barely registered the viaduct's looming presence – probably because I was too lost in my own preoccupations to use my eyes. Dwellers in the capital tend to take their surroundings for granted, and often need a shift in perception to get re-engaged.

I received a jolt of this kind during a recent ride up Bishopsgate on the top deck of a 135 bus. As we swung into Great Eastern Street, I noticed something I'd never spotted before: part of the raised Victorian trackbed that once carried trains to and from the North London Railway's terminus at Broad Street. It's been starkly amputated on the southern side of the road; but opposite, the railway's former presence has been marked more lovingly by the Village Underground's Holywell Lane centre for 'creativity and culture', where graffiti-decorated tube train carriages stand at the height of the old tracks on what appear to be modified shipping containers. I was eager to get up to their level and look at things from their perspective; and though access to the Village Underground site itself proved impossible, despite repeated requests, I was able to experience this higher, calmer viewpoint by taking a train ride along the Kingsland Viaduct – formerly connected to the demolished Holywell Lane/Great Eastern Street route into Broad Street, but still in use by the Overground. To do so, I followed the viaduct north at street level as far as Hoxton station, where I climbed the stairs for the short journey back to Shoreditch High Street.

From the platform at Hoxton, the viaduct seemed generously wide, in spacious contrast to the streets and pavements below. My train glided in and headed south, providing voyeuristic glimpses through the upper windows of surrounding buildings. The Victorian brickwork supporting the permanent way was interspersed with metal bridges over the roads; it merged, almost seamlessly, into the recent stretch of track that leads across the High Street and towards the new station. Here, the spacious feel was lost; but a partial view of the Braithwaite viaduct, just before the train arrived at the boxed-in platforms, made me keen to see more of this area - if possible, from an even higher position.

An opportunity to do so arose when we obtained permission to visit the roof of Bishopsgate's 540-foot-high Broadgate Tower - completed in 2009, and an elegantly dominant presence on the skyline when seen from the southbound platform at Hoxton station. Closer, at its base, the Tower gives a different impression: a sense of braced mass and glossy solidity. It's the latest in a long line of celebrated architecture around here. In July 1840, the inauguration of the still-unfinished Bishopsgate station (admired for its Italianate style and the "lightness and simplicity" of its corrugated iron roof[7]) was marked by "the firing of cannon, and attended by a band of music";[8] while in 1881, the goods yard that obliterated it made an even greater impact with its elegant wrought-iron gates and brick- and terracotta-dressed windows. The Victorians were unsentimental about destroying old and unwanted buildings in order to accommodate new ones. They probably pulled down the fine passenger terminus at Bishopsgate almost as readily as they disposed of the "large numbers of old houses of the most frail and shanty-like character"[9] that also stood in the way of the 1881 depot; and they spared Braithwaite's viaduct simply because it was operationally essential.

Nowadays, there's a host of regulations to minimise such destruction, and ensure that the views of existing historical structures aren't spoiled by new developments. The creation of the Broadgate Tower has been described as "a work of negotiation and manoeuvre"[10] around such legal and planning obstacles. It occupies "a plot shaped by historic vagaries of land ownership, scooped out underneath by the railway tracks heading into Liverpool Street station";[11] significantly, work on it was delayed for some time when a number of archeological finds were uncovered, and had to be painstakingly removed and documented.

Initially, we found the view from its roof overwhelming, and briefly lost our bearings until the sight of the Thames brought things back into place. Paradoxically, the streets closest to the base of the Tower were invisible or obscured to us at this height, though farther-away locations were crystal clear. The river stretched off eastwards; tall London buildings, old and new, seemed shrunken and humbled; while the Kingsland Viaduct was a prominent, snaking presence to the north. But almost immediately, our eyes were held by the Bishopsgate goods yard. With its heights and depths harder to make out with the naked eye (though restored in the photographs), its most striking features were those of texture, colour and shape: the ochre and turquoise of its sports pitches; the garish patches of graffiti; and most of all, the lush green, broken up by barren, bald seams, of the Braithwaite Viaduct itself. What did those strips of wilderness resemble? Maybe a degree of light-headedness affected us as we gazed downwards; we were a long way from the ground, after all. I'd previously read that the outline of the ruins was like "a leg of mutton", and when I'd seen an old aerial photograph of the goods yard with its roof in place, taken before the 1964 fire, it had reminded me of a washboard. From the top of Broadgate Tower, I thought the raised viaduct area appeared to be coffin-shaped, or like the magnet of an electric guitar pickup surrounded by broken windings. Olivia's notions were stranger: a medieval stringed instrument...a shard of bismuth...and even a tiger hissing cockroach!

One creature that didn't immediately come to mind was a beached whale, but the goods yard is certainly washed up and stranded in its current, derelict state - disconnected from the energy of the trains flowing nearby, and overlaid and surrounded by sardonic graffiti ("NO Good REASON", screams a sign over the cutting that serves Liverpool Street). I began to explore it at ground level on a summer day several weeks later; and as I walked around its perimeter, my memory of how it had looked from above proved a more effective guide than a map. Up close, however, there were erosions and accretions one could reach out and touch, as well as areas beneath the viaduct's arches that were invisible from the air.

Nature abhors a vacuum, and people, if they aren't prevented, can't resist leaving their mark on any accessible, unadorned surface. Individually, the 'love locks' on a wire fence in what's now Braithwaite Street seemed small, polite, even poignant. Seen en masse, they were incongruous and untidy, though they provided a colourful clash with the drab barriers and metal gates that proliferate here. The hoardings on the side of the viaduct near the sports pitches were also unlovely, but at least they obscured the crumbling stonework, birds' nests, and bags of rubbish within the bare arches farther along. Where the road passes underneath the viaduct – according to local boy and *Crazy Gang* star Bud Flanagan (1896-1968), dancers used to come here to practise their steps to mouth-organ accompaniment - there was a smell of urine and evidence of rough sleeping. When the goods yard was intact, this covered area was much longer, and it attracted a greater number of homeless Londoners: in Victorian times, destitute children were rescued from it by the Scottish evangelical Quaker, philanthropist and fervent hymn-singer Annie MacPherson.

The neighbourhood is no longer so notorious for its deprivation and crime, but the current guardians of the goods yard are suspicious about loiterers, and there was a proliferation of 'keep out' notices, erected by 'Land Sheriffs' who clearly meant business.

NO UNAUTHORISED PERSON
PERMITTED ON THESE LANDS
WITHOUT WRITTEN PERMISSION

Their stern tone was an invitation to mischief, and there was plenty to be seen around here - most prominently, the 'Fame/Sex' signs dangling from a lamp post, and the neatly amended information board, just down the road near the old Shoreditch tube station, welcoming visitors to 'Alien Gardens.'

Over time, what's actually Allen Gardens, east of Brick Lane, has been adjoined and criss-crossed, like a piano frame, by past and present train tracks. Some of these metals are still in place, singing and rustling as the trains run along them, but others are gone. The railway bridge to Bishopsgate across Brick Lane itself was dismantled long ago. The East London underground service ran nearby, but closed in 2006, and the cutting that led into its old terminus was subsequently filled in. The Overground, operating from Shoreditch High Street, has replaced it, and takes a different route into and above the Gardens; but the discarded tube station building still stands, covered in graffiti: when we photographed it, it was serving as a makeshift cinema. And a little to the east - nestling between the Overground, starting its climb towards Shoreditch High Street, and the lines serving Liverpool Street – is a patch of land that puzzled us when we saw it from the Tower: it's a Nomadic Community Garden, growing plants and vegetables, and displaying a range of curious, stimulating artwork.

I concluded my walk around the edge of the goods yard by heading up Brick Lane, left into Sclater Street, and on to the junction with Bethnal Green Road before the turn back into Braithwaite Street. I couldn't ignore the viaduct, or the surviving sections of the depot's outer wall, as I once did; teasing fragments of toys, dolls and other odd little items embedded in the brickwork constantly drew me over for a closer look. Though these knick-knacks, like the love locks and the weeds, are parasites (or saprophytes) - further signs of the viaduct and yard's ongoing ruination − I was perversely pleased by their presence, at least in the summer weather. But my whimsical attraction to the site in its current, mouldering state was lessened when I came back on a damp December evening, and didn't enjoy what I saw or heard. Padlocks and doll fragments may not be to everyone's taste, but amplified pre-Christmas busking has a far more toxic effect on an area's ambience. And the two drunken loudmouths I encountered under the viaduct that night ("BIG MAN! BIG MAN!") were sorry successors to William Penn, Annie MacPherson, or Bud Flanagan's dancers. Travelling in on the bus, I'd been cleaning my spectacles with a disposable cloth saturated (according to its label) in 'denatured alcohol', and I wondered whether the music and shouting were some sort of aural equivalent to this substance, swabbing the character from a place, and leaving it smeared and poisoned.

The jury is still out on Shoreditch's future shape: at the time of writing, it was being reported that the then London Mayor, Boris Johnson - whose predecessor, Ken Livingstone, famously dismissed the goods yard as "a load of old crap"[12] - would be the ultimate arbiter on pending plans for it. Whatever happens, the developers will be held to their promise to show respect for its "existing materiality, patina and atmosphere",[13] but however this is done, the place will change forever: the viaduct will still be there, but the unkempt mystery that's so impressive from the air, and at street level in summer, will probably be tidied out of existence. And what, for me, are the strangest, most haunted parts of it - the oddly lit interiors within the fences; the alcove adopted as a makeshift berth by a homeless man − will almost certainly vanish as well. No rational case could be made for their retention as part of a designer's 'fit-out', and I can't imagine how they might they be described, let alone assigned a purpose or function, in a policy document. I'm glad we were able to see them, and record them on film: such views may be tantalising and partial, but they are revealing in ways that are hard to put into words.

The Village Underground site, with its mural by Stephen Powers

The Braithwaite Viaduct from ground level

The viaduct, its hoardings, fences and sports pitches. Braithwaite Street runs through it

Left: The vibrantly decorated
entrance to the old Shoreditch
Underground station
Above: Love locks adorn the fencing
in Braithwaite Street
Below: Toys embedded in the wall
beside Sclater Street

Mischief in the air:
the 'Fame/Sex' street lamp…

…plus a neatly amended sign, and a
'shoe tree' with a difference!

Underneath the viaduct…

'Buffer Stops Moorgate': the line beyond them to Lothbury was never built

THE CITY'S UNBUILT RAIL ROUTE

Mr. Charles Pooter, the central character in George and Weedon Grossmith's sublimely funny depiction of late Victorian London life, *The Diary of a Nobody*,[14] is a middle-aged City clerk with thinning hair and a soft beard. Six days a week, he catches an omnibus from Holloway (where he shares a rented house with his "dear wife Carrie" and their insolent son, Lupin) to his office; one morning, he narrowly avoids a reprimand from his boss, Mr. Perkupp, after missing the quarter-to-nine service, and arriving half an hour late.

Pooter's home, 'The Laurels', is described and illustrated in some detail, and a recent article for *The Spectator* by Harry Mount identifies the real-life property that may have inspired it. It's in Pemberton Gardens, Upper Holloway: "an end-of-terrace...[with] little front and back gardens and ten steps leading up to the front door."[15] Upper Holloway railway station opened in 1868, and served a line running towards Gospel Oak that wouldn't have been especially convenient for a City commuter like Pooter - who, in any case, seems to have taken a dim view of trains: in the book, he obtains a £2 rent reduction after complaining to his landlord about the nuisance caused by them. But a brisk walk southeast down Holloway Road would have brought his real-life counterparts close to Drayton Park, which, in 1904, became an open-air stop on the Great Northern & City's otherwise mostly underground route between Finsbury Park and Moorgate Street (now Moorgate) stations. Journeys between the two took thirteen minutes, just as they do now.

As its name suggests, the GN&C was meant to link up with the Great Northern's Hertfordshire services at Finsbury Park, enabling them to run into Moorgate Street; and its tunnels were built large and wide enough to "take the [Great Northern's] heaviest suburban trains."[16] But the Great Northern changed its mind about the connection, and the GN&C found itself excluded from the main part of Finsbury Park station, having to operate instead from an inconvenient underground platform.

There were other disappointments and embarrassments for the little line. Its launch, on 14th February 1904, was poorly publicised: "it was some time before the people in the district knew that [it] was open."[17] Early financial results were bad, and during the first few months of operation, a "stoppage of traffic" was caused by "rats eating the rubber casing of a cable and setting up a short circuit."[18] Two years before, the GN&C had been given permission to extend its metals and tunnels 270 yards south from Moorgate to a new station, named Lothbury, near the Bank of England. The plan was popular with commuters, who began voicing their displeasure when it failed to materialise. Mr. Henry Smith of Mountgrove Road in Highbury summed up their feelings in a letter to the *London Daily News* that could have been penned by Charles Pooter himself.

"The distance [from Moorgate Street to Lothbury] may be short, but [the extension] would be a great boon to those who reside in North London. It is very irritating to have to change and take the City and South London Tube *[now the Northern Line]* with consequent waste of time in the very narrow staircase. The missing link would be a great convenience..."[19]

Sufficient funds couldn't be raised for the project, and it had to be abandoned. Part of the Greathead shield that would have excavated the tunnel to Lothbury was left in the wall beyond the buffers at the southern end of Moorgate Street's Platform 10, and seems to be still there today.

The GN&C's proprietors did their best to promote a positive image of the line in the press. In October 1903, they had promised that Lothbury station would boast "a novelty in the shape of a moving staircase to convey passengers to and from the surface."[20] And in 1906, it was announced that "smoking carriages on [their] trains have been fitted with penny-in-the-slot machines containing cigarettes and matches, whilst the 'non-smokers' are provided with similar machines filled with sweetmeats. The first train had to be refilled on its arrival at its destination..."[21] But in 1913, despite brave efforts to retain its independence, the GN&C was acquired by the Metropolitan Railway company, which pledged that "the whole system of the line [would] be overhauled and the stations renovated."[22] Twenty years later, when the London Passenger Transport Board took over management of the Metropolitan, the Finsbury Park-Moorgate route was renamed the Northern City Line, and was soon being shown in 'Northern Line' black on Underground maps. It was later known as the Highbury Branch, and, in 1964, Drayton Park (from where there's a continuous tunnel to Moorgate) became its northern terminus.

At about 8.45 on the morning of Friday 28th February 1975, a six-car, southbound Underground service from Drayton Park, carrying some 300 passengers, was approaching Moorgate's Platform 9. It was common practice for drivers ('motormen') to reduce or shut off their trains' traction power while still outside the station, and then apply the brakes so as to come into the platform at about 10 mph, making it easy to stop. But for some reason, this train failed to slow down. It entered Moorgate at approximately 35 mph, ran through the sand drag beyond the southern end of the platform (designed to contain the impact of a slow-speed overrun), and collided first with a buffer, and then with the end wall of the tunnel. The "first and second cars of the train and the front portion of the third car [were] crushed into approximately half their normal length,"[23] and 43 people were killed - including the driver, who, according to witnesses, had been "sitting upright and looking forward"[24] in the cab as it sped into the station. There were 74 injuries. The train had been in good working order, and the motorman was described by colleagues as "cautious but competent," and "a cheerful chap" who had seemed "absolutely normal and fit"[25] earlier that morning. The disaster was undoubtedly due to his actions, but "whether [these were] deliberate or...the result of a suddenly arising physical condition not revealed [by a] post-mortem examination, there [was] not sufficient evidence to establish."[26]

The Moorgate accident was a tragic final episode in the Underground's long stewardship of the Highbury Branch. In October 1975, the line was temporarily closed in order to re-convert it to regular train use, and in August 1976, it began, at last, to function as its creators had intended. 'Great Northern Electrics' ran direct between Moorgate and destinations in Hertfordshire via the main line platforms at Finsbury Park. They operated from Monday to Friday until December 2015, when seven-day working was introduced. There are current plans to "improve station facilities and appearance",[27] and to introduce new, air-conditioned trains.

***

I'm not sure whether the map co-ordinates I found on the Internet for the non-existent GN&C terminus at Lothbury were quite accurate. They point to a spot so close to the Old Lady of Threadneedle Street's stony skirts that it's hard to imagine a railway station there. Lothbury, though, would certainly have benefitted City workers eager to avoid the road congestion of a London rush hour. Even with no latter-day Mr. Perkupp to chivvy me, I found myself growing impatient with crowds and traffic lights on my short walk from here to Moorgate station – a place whose awkward layout and confusing signage often lead to further delays and confusions. After a couple of wrong turnings along its passageways, I found my way down to platforms 9 and 10, the arrival and departure point for 'Great Northern inner suburban services.'

This part of Moorgate has a gloomy, brooding mood that's as contagious as a virus; on a previous visit, I remember being so infected by it that I failed to notice a friend waving at me from a few feet away. The 'slanting flash' livery on its walls - a hangover from Network SouthEast days before the privatisation of British Rail in 1994 - accentuates its dated look; and despite the cosmetic changes to passages and platforms, middle-aged Londoners like me can't help recalling the 1975 disaster when we pass through.

I had a student job as a City clerk back then, though, unlike Mr. Pooter, I was only a junior temp, and a barely competent one at that. I don't recollect the name or exact location of the company that employed me, but it can't have been especially close to Moorgate station, as I travelled in via Liverpool Street. We started work at 10.00 am, so the crash had already occurred before I arrived that February morning, and I saw no ambulances and heard no sirens to alert me to it. In those days, we didn't have TVs, computers, mobiles, or even transistor radios in the office, and only found out what had happened when a wave of anxious phone calls began coming in from our families and friends, checking that we were OK. Ordinarily, these would have been frowned upon by the bosses – one of whom had warned me, on my first day, not to bring a cup of coffee over to my desk, "or there'd be a revolution" - but nothing was said in the exceptional circumstances, and I think we all left early, reading the *Evening Standard* and *Evening News* accounts of what had happened as we headed home.

Seeking to dismiss these dismal memories, I focused instead on the final few yards of the Platform 10 tunnel. They're referred to officially as 'Buffer Stops Moorgate', and peering at them from near the tail of my waiting train gave me a pleasing sense of intrusion upon a 'backstage' area. The buffers themselves seemed oddly flimsy, unlike the succession of formidable metal rings that reinforce the tunnel's roof and sides and lead back to its rear wall, where I could see what appeared to be the remains of the Greathead shield.

It was time to get onboard the dirty old 'electrical multiple unit' (EMU) that had been ticking insistently beside me. The signal cleared, the engine revved up, and we lurched off into the darkness. The next two stops, Old Street and Essex Road, were dingy and sparsely populated, but my spirits lifted as we came into the daylight at Drayton Park, where I disembarked to observe a curious ritual involving the train.

The station has an island platform, with an official notice to railway staff at its southern end: 'Northern City Line Procedures start beyond K360/K358 Signal and Buffer Stops Moorgate.' These procedures include the use of a third-rail power supply in the tunnel I'd just passed through. Once above ground, though, the third-rail system is replaced by overhead electrical cables, and trains must connect to them by raising their roof-mounted pantographs. While watching the switchover, I found myself fantasising about its possible portrayal on a wildlife-style TV programme. There'd be a *sotto voce* commentary, and a cameraman would be in position to capture the slow upward extension of the metal arm, followed by the sparky kiss of its contact with the wires. We'd hear a subtle pitch change in the humming motors, and then the coaches would roll out of Drayton Park...escaping the city with an exhilarating whoosh that might have disconcerted Charles Pooter (who was "rather afraid"[28] of the noise from the locomotives near his house), but would have been recognised by an only slightly later, but far more adventurous commentator, Futurist artist and musician Luigi Russolo, as part of "the variety of din" we encounter when we "cross a great modern capital with our ears more alert than our eyes."[29]

Looking east along the island platform at Drayton Park

A train's pantograph being raised to connect with the overhead wires

Discolouration and sprouting plants on the brickwork of the Goodman's Fields viaduct

GOODMAN'S FIELDS VIADUCT AND 'THE TILBURY'

When the London & Blackwall Railway east from Minories opened in July 1840 (its western terminus at Fenchurch Street came into use the following year), it was drawn by ropes powered by stationary steam-engines. A magazine article published just after its launch hoped it would reduce the number of "ponderous sugar-wagons and their long, heavy teams toiling up the roads of [the] neighbourhood", and also predicted: "Its passenger transit will, doubtless, be very considerable."[30] An extension to Bow began operating in 1849, and standard locomotives were introduced at the same time. In the 1850s, agreements and connections with the Eastern Counties Railway helped to boost the L&B's commuter traffic, as did the launch of the London, Tilbury & Southend company, initially as a joint venture with the ECR.

Later, trains from the new docks at Tilbury were able to deliver their freight (wool, livestock and a range of other imports, including Christmas turkeys) via a short, specially constructed spur from the L&B lines to a huge depot in Goodman's Fields, off the Commercial Road, with a bonded warehouse above it. The depot opened, simultaneously with the docks, in April 1886, but the warehouse wasn't ready until the following year, and revenues from the goods brought into London from Tilbury were initially disappointing. A newspaper reported that summer: "There is some talk of 'boycotting' [the recently opened docks]...[but] the simple truth appears to be that merchants prefer to have their cargoes near to hand."[31]

The depot building, rapidly nicknamed the 'Tilbury', was characterised by East End chronicler Ed Glinert as "strictly utilitarian industrial architecture."[32] It achieved notoriety as a makeshift, insalubrious bomb shelter during the London Blitz that began in September 1940. Its vast underground spaces were intended to harbour no more than 3,000 people, but on some nights, at least 14,000 would take refuge there. By all accounts, the place was a hell-hole. To quote Glinert again, "[its] floor space was broken up by a network of archways, and platforms four feet from the ground ran along the length of the basement."[33] Henry Moore, who captured it in the sketches and paintings he produced as an official war artist, described it as "dramatic, dismal lit, [with] masses of reclining figures fading to perspective point."[34] Feliks Topolski, also working as a war artist, created a more savagely energetic image of it, with a pair of whirling dancers in the foreground, in his *Safety Quarters for the Hoi Polloi*, drawn in 1940. And we have vivid written testimony of its cramped, stinking conditions from *Daily Herald* journalist Ritchie Calder...

"I have seen some of the worst haunts on the waterfront at Marseilles which are a byword, but they were mild compared with the cesspool of humanity which welled into that shelter...Prostitutes paraded [inside]. Hawkers peddled greasy, cold, fried fish which cloyed the already foul atmosphere. Free fights had to be broken up by the police."[35]

...and from Nina Masel, a diarist for the Mass-Observation social research project who later (as Nina Hibbin) became a film critic for the *Daily Worker* and *Morning Star*:

"The first time I went in there, I had to come out, I felt sick. You just couldn't see anything, you could just smell the fug, the overwhelming stench...There were thousands and thousands of people lying head to toe, all along the bays...[and] at the beginning, there were only four earth buckets down the far end, behind screens, for toilets."[36]

By the time King George VI and U.S. First Lady Eleanor Roosevelt visited the Tilbury in October 1942, sanitation and other essentials had been slightly improved. Other distinguished guests included the Soviet ambassador Ivan Maisky and American presidential candidate Wendell Willkie, and there was also a stream of "socially curious sightseers, 'slummers' [from wealthier parts of London] on a new version of a pub-crawl."[37] Plays and concerts were put on there too, and in December 1941, the *Daily Mirror* carried a touching photograph, headlined "Interior decorations – unlimited",[38] of children amusing themselves by drawing on its walls.

The depot closed in 1967, and was subsequently demolished. The line that linked it to the elevated railway tracks now used by c2c and the DLR has also been removed, but the curved viaduct near Shadwell (the 'Goodman's Fields Viaduct') that supported its first few yards is still a significant presence at street and track level. When I had my initial glimpse of it, from a train carriage, I was intrigued by its grassy top, and wanted to take a closer, stationary look - though I knew that getting to it from the main line would be tricky, and wondered whether its 'roof' could be reached more easily and safely from below, maybe via a staircase or hatch.

As I knew little about its location - Pinchin Street, off Back Church Lane - I got hold of some old maps, and compared them to modern street plans before checking the area out from the road. Unlike its ruined cousin at Bishopsgate, the viaduct has fairly well preserved brickwork, despite some moss, moisture and discolouration; and many of its arches are occupied by prosperous small businesses. Such admirable tenants are very different from their Victorian forebears. Back then, viaducts were undesirable places, frequently used for cheap overnight accommodation; in the words of one East Ender, quoted in 1846, they "would not be tolerated in a respectable neighbourhood, and undoubtedly render[ed] a bad one worse."[39] This viaduct, too, has a shady past, connected to 19th century London's most enduring and unsavoury murder mystery. A dismembered and decomposing torso, thought to be that of a victim of Jack the Ripper, was discovered beneath it on 10th September 1889, wrapped in sacking. Death, in a politer, more discreet form, still hangs around here: one of the arches is occupied by an undertaker, and houses a 'private ambulance' of the type that transports corpses.

But for all the bustling activity inside and alongside the structure, and its proximity to the busy train lines running close by, its *raison d'être* as a route to the old depot and warehouse has gone, and there are telltale symptoms of this redundancy. Wild plants dangle over its sides, and burst out more exuberantly from its cut-off western end. The four-storey Tilbury stood only a short distance away, between Gower's Walk to the east and a thoroughfare called Lambeth Street to the west: the now-dismantled tracks would have turned northwards and crossed Back Church Lane to reach it.

At the time of writing, heavy construction work is underway near Gower's Walk, and while there is probably little nostalgia for the depot itself, people who live and work here are concerned that their historic surroundings may be threatened by "insensitive transformation"[40] and dense development. There are even fears for the viaduct's future, as we learned when we began shooting, and met Jenni Boswell-Jones, whose ArtZone co-operative actually has an office within it.

Jenni and her husband, artist Ismail Saray, have been acting as voluntary managers for its 'roof' - which, they told us, had been given additional protection by being designated a 'Site of Importance for Nature Conservation' (SINC) - and thanks to them and to John Archer (Tower Hamlets Council's Biodiversity Officer), we were able to access it, though my notion of doing so via a flight of stairs or through a hatch was off the mark. The only way up and down was on a ladder, placed in the yard outside ArtZone's offices. Various uneasy thoughts passed through my mind as I began to climb it, but the rungs were sturdy, and took us fairly swiftly onto the grassy plateau parallel to the railway line.

Up here, nature was certainly in evidence - even taking hold. Among the railway junk that littered the ground was a selection of flourishing flora, its seeds spread by birds, and by the foxes that need no ladders for their visits. The furrows they'd made in the grass were clear to see, and one animal had left behind a well-chewed red ball. Other, more unsightly refuse had been carefully gathered together by Ismail, who'd also set up a makeshift but robust pulley close to where our ladder was propped.

We peered over the viaduct's western edge: the sprouting flowers there had been invisible from below. Walking to its other end, we photographed the spot where the railway lines start to split away towards Shadwell, and stared down at the bulky machinery in the yard; the Gap plant hire firm is among ArtZone's fellow tenants, and, at the time, its distinctive banner festooned the side of the viaduct visible from the railway. Our overwhelming sensation was one of pleasing disorientation. We had an opportunity to see tracks and trains from a fresh angle, and to get a steady, static look at the upper storeys of nearby buildings, quite unlike the snatched views obtained on a train ride. Some of these structures, of course, stand directly between the viaduct and the site of the old warehouse and depot, and as the street layout has changed since the days of the Tilbury, the route once taken by the spur is hard to visualise. Its departure point remains with us, but despite its enduring solidity, it's being increasingly encroached upon – from one side, by trackside paraphernalia and railway materials; and, from the other, by new building schemes that Jenni, Ismail and their supporters have so far managed to oppose. I'm sure they will use their best efforts to protect the viaduct...which, to fantasise for a moment, strikes me as a pleasingly unconventional (if impractical and undoubtedly illegal) location for a 'sundowner.' I can picture myself, equipped with a deckchair, a parasol and a cold beer, lounging beside the tracks up there, toasting the bewildered commuters as they speed past.

The viaduct from the street, and at track level

The entrance to what was once the 'London Necropolis' railway station

121 WESTMINSTER BRIDGE ROAD: 'THE SALLY PORT TO ETERNITY'

Because I could not stop for Death -
He kindly stopped for me -
The Carriage held but just Ourselves -
And Immortality.

The encounter with Death in Emily Dickinson's poem is disquieting: but at least the carriage she describes is private, appropriately slow-moving, and drawn by horses - though not ones of flesh and blood. Victorian Londoners often had to make do with faster, less exclusive ways of transporting their dead; the city's burial practices were changing, due to a rising population, and limited space in its graveyards. At a meeting in Blackfriars in November 1849, The National Society for the Abolition of Burials in Towns called for "common land in the neighbourhood of railways" around the capital to be "appropriated for general cemeteral purposes", and suggested that "sidings or branch lines" should be constructed nearby "[to accommodate] funeral trains."[41]

Such controversial ideas had attracted the disapproval of the Bishop of London, Charles Blomfield, at a Parliamentary select committee hearing seven years earlier. The bishop considered the "hurry and bustle" of train travel "inconsistent with the solemnity of a Christian funeral", and was offended by the prospect of the mortal remains of "some respectable member of the church" being carried alongside those of a "profligate spendthrift."[42] Nevertheless, the demand for so-called 'extramural burials' proved irresistible, and the London Necropolis Company, established in 1850, was to be their best-known provider.

The firm supplied everything necessary for an out-of-town funeral, from dedicated rail links to moderately priced "coffins, attendants, and every other furniture for interments"[43] - dealing "a sad blow to the metropolitan undertakers", in the words of the *Surrey Comet.*[44] The first burials at its 'Cemetery Beautiful' in Brookwood, near Woking, took place in November 1854. Corpses and mourners travelled the 25 miles from the capital on special trains drawn by London & South Western Railway locomotives. They used private stations: departures were initially from a terminus near Leake Street, beside Waterloo, and in February 1902, the LNC moved to new, larger premises on Westminster Bridge Road.

The concept of a "railway system of interment" attracted heavy mockery in the press. *Punch* magazine commented, in September 1859: "We have very often heard of railways having killed people, but we never before learnt that they undertook to bury them...They have buried heaps of money, there is no denying

39

that; and they have also caused interment of the hopes of many shareholders. These burials have been generally performed at railroad speed; nevertheless we think their rapid execution can hardly be regarded as an act of happy dispatch."[45]

But there was also considerable curiosity, bordering on the ghoulish, about the LNC's operations, and in April 1902, an unctuous description of its Westminster Bridge Road headquarters appeared in the *London Daily News*. "The old depot on the north side of the railway [has been] swallowed up for the use of the iron horse, and in its place has been built quite a palatial station on the south side...It need only be said that it is designed and furnished with the same sympathy that is conspicuous in every place which comes under the control of the company...The arrangements ensure complete privacy for the funerals. Directly the [hearse] carriages pass through the archway [beside the main road] they are beyond the public gaze, and the glass-roofed station yard, with its white tiled walls and rows of palms and bay trees, produces anything but a morbid effect."[46]

There were doorways from the yard into a now-vanished building that contained mortuaries, workshops and storage areas. Its top floor led to the company's 1st and 3rd class railway platforms, as well as waiting rooms for passengers accompanying the deceased to Brookwood, and a richly appointed *chapelle ardente* where a coffin could rest, surrounded by candles and flanked by mourners, before being loaded onto a train. The lines from the Necropolis station joined the main LSWR tracks just outside Waterloo; after the 'Grouping' of 1923, the LSWR became part of the Southern Railway.

The irreverent nicknames bestowed on the daily Westminster Bridge Road to Brookwood service - 'Stiffs' Express', the 'Black Line' - contrasted with the solemn rectitude of the London Necropolis Company itself. Its telegraphic address was "*Tenebratio, London*",[47] its letters and documents were heavy with gothic type, and one can picture its employees, like the funeral directors' mutes in Charles Dickens' *Martin Chuzzlewit*, "looking as mournful as could be reasonably expected of men with such a thriving job in hand."[48] In fact, the company never quite achieved the dominance hoped for by its ambitious founders - though Brookwood was, for a while, the largest burial ground in the world, and the LNC undoubtedly brought new levels of dignified efficiency to the gloomy task of organising interments among its picturesque "trees, flowers and winding paths."[49] However, as new cemeteries opened around London, and the use of road hearses powered by internal combustion engines grew,[50] traffic from Westminster Bridge Road fell, slowly but steadily. The station was almost totally destroyed by Luftwaffe bombs on April 16th 1941, and was never used again. The LNC surrendered its lease on the premises after the end of the war, and the firm was eventually taken over - though Brookwood remains open to visitors, and for burials.

***

Westminster Bridge House (121 Westminster Bridge Road), from where the London Necropolis Company was run, has survived more-or-less intact, but extensive demolition and redevelopment are underway beside it, and its entrance is formidably barred. At the time of writing, the building seemed to be unoccupied: its lifelessness was in stark contrast to the constant noise from the site next door, and the busy traffic on the A23 just outside. It was hard to imagine the place in its heyday, when substantial numbers of mourners would sometimes arrive to accompany the 'great and the good' being buried at Brookwood. One of the largest of such gatherings was in honour of Father Arthur Stanton, the much-loved 'slum priest' who died in March 1913. Following a Requiem Mass at St. Alban's, Holborn, where Stanton had served as curate for half a century, a procession more than a mile long escorted his bier down Kingsway, and across Waterloo Bridge to the Necropolis Station. "The streets were lined with reverent and attentive spectators", and some 800 people took the train with the coffin.[51]

There are no memorials to this and countless other final journeys here, other than the well preserved brick and terracotta façade of Westminster Bridge House itself. Olivia's camera was able to capture its intricacies, and could peer in through the railings at the elegant curves and fine tiles of the reception office; but without some sort of magical, endoscope-like lens attachment, it was impossible to stand at the gate and look around the corner into the yard where the hearses used to unload. Fortunately, we later found a different vantage point from which we could see and photograph this carefully secluded spot.

A nearby walkway was as close as we could get, without trespassing, to where the LNC's platforms and waiting rooms would have stood. It afforded an excellent view down into the back yard of Westminster Bridge House; in the other direction were fenced off train tracks and other railway equipment, and beyond them, the junction with the main line out of Waterloo.

I'd already seen some of this hinterland from what I'd caught myself thinking of as 'the other side' - actually the lefthand window of an outbound train – but our new standpoint was a better, though potentially misleading one...for the old terminus is completely gone. I'd studied the photographs taken after the 1941 bomb attack upon it – showing twisted, broken tracks and girders, and a wrecked carriage at a crazy angle on top of them – and read John M. Clarke's descriptions, based on contemporary records, of what was destroyed then, and dismantled later. He tells us that "much of the station, waiting rooms, *chapelle ardente*, workshops, [and] caretakers' flats"[52] were wiped out by the Luftwaffe. A National Railway Museum photo shows the platforms still in position in 1948, but they, too, have since vanished, and the original rails were taken up decades ago. Today's site is like a table that's been re-laid long after the departure of the guests who once sat, stood or were carried there. Its electricity substations, spiked barriers and powerful lights are all standard railway siding components, set out in place of items that have rotted away, been blown up, or just removed. A few may have a pseudo-1940s look, such as the brick outbuilding adjacent to one of the lines, or the pulley contraption with a safe working limit (SWL) of 5 hundredweight - strong enough to shift a stack of coffins - but none of them has any relation to the facilities for the 'Stiffs' Express', most of whose elements have been as utterly obliterated as flesh from the bodies on a Parsi Tower of Silence. Those sombre places (with their demarcated pathways, and separate trenches for the corpses of men, women and children) were as meticulously segregated as the LNC's stations and cemetery – though the bare bones left behind on the Towers were eventually swept into a single pit, while at Brookwood, divisions of class and religious belief are eternally perpetuated by discrete burial plots.

I find myself reaching for these odd analogies because the lost Necropolis terminus is like nothing else I know, and because the procedures associated with it seem so curious now. But its location above the streets of Waterloo wasn't as high, or as quiet, as a Tower of Silence's, so perhaps the first-ever phrase the station suggested to me is still the most appropriate. It's from D.K. Broster's Jacobite novel *The Gleam in the North* (1927): she used it to describe a gallows, but it seems fitting for this unsettling place, in which no one – living or dead – would wish to linger very long: "The sally port to Eternity."

The reception office behind the entrance gates of 121 Westminster Bridge Road. To its right is the driveway leading inwards

The rear of the driveway, and the tracks connecting to the main line from Waterloo

Office units, graffiti and railway hardware - but no trace of the Necropolis platforms

The remains of the Limehouse Curve, seen from the Accumulator Tower

MIDDLE ZONE

THE LIMEHOUSE CURVE

Is London really a series of 'villages'? Country dwellers usually know their little communities like the backs of their hands, but residents of the capital are rarely so familiar with the streets where they live. I'm constantly surprised and confused by my own 'manor', Docklands: a shiny new district, built upon the remnants of a mighty imperial port whose truncated fragments are still scattered all around.

A few of the area's once significant structures have vanished completely, like the first Limehouse railway station, which closed in 1926. It lay well to the east of its modern successor - close to a Grade II-listed bridge that's been blocked in by recent building on Lowell Street, across Commercial Road. The bridge's top is now overgrown and fenced off, as can be seen from the DLR (which follows the course of the old London & Blackwall Railway here). It formerly carried the first section of the 500-yard 'Limehouse Curve', completed in 1880, and linking the L&B (leased, by then, to the Great Eastern) to a junction at Salmon Lane that's now on the route taken by c2c trains out of Fenchurch Street. The Curve was part of a £300,000 package of improvements announced by the Great Eastern in 1878,[53] and it provided an efficient, time-saving path for goods traffic from the docks, where 'big steamers' like the ones celebrated in Rudyard Kipling's poem were already delivering ever-growing volumes of cargo.

> "OH, where are you going to, all you Big Steamers,
> With England's own coal, up and down the salt seas?"
> "We are going to fetch you your bread and your butter,
> Your beef, pork, and mutton, eggs, apples, and cheese."
>
> "And where will you fetch it from, all you Big Steamers,
> And where shall I write you when you are away?"
> "We fetch it from Melbourne, Quebec, and Vancouver.
> Address us at Hobart, Hong-kong, and Bombay."
>
> "But if anything happened to all you Big Steamers,
> And suppose you were wrecked up and down the salt sea?"
> "Why, you'd have no coffee or bacon for breakfast,
> And you'd have no muffins or toast for your tea."

[...]

"For the bread that you eat and the biscuits you nibble,
The sweets that you suck and the joints that you carve,
They are brought to you daily by All Us Big Steamers
And if any one hinders our coming you'll starve!"[54]

Big Steamers was commissioned for a school text-book and published in 1911, well before London's docks had attained their peak capacity. By their heyday in the 1930s, they were handling 35 million tons of cargo a year, worth £700 million.[55] Some of it – like the bananas from the Caribbean that the 'Fyffes Line' had begun to import prior to World War I – needed careful treatment, and Fyffes' steamers had specially cooled holds to keep their bananas firm and fresh. On arrival at the docks, the delicate produce would be transferred to railway 'banana vans', and sent on its way, often via the nearby Limehouse Curve.

Though the Curve was sometimes used by passenger services (and, latterly, by railway enthusiasts' excursions), it was primarily for freight, and its fortunes were inextricably bound up with those of the docks. Their decline in the 1950s and 60s, as the massive container ships that had superseded Kipling's 'big steamers' headed for ports with greater capacity, meant that the little link was no longer cost-effective, and it carried its last-ever train on 5th November 1962.

***

Close to the stub of the Limehouse Curve is a riverside site, once known as the Regent's Canal Dock, whose slow decay had preceded that of the London docks. Opened in 1820, and popular in Victorian times with steamers serving British and foreign destinations, it was also the entry point for goods being transferred from the Thames onto the Regent's Canal and the network of man-made waterways that lay beyond it. Railways and roads eventually took away much of this traffic, and the Dock – despite having once boasted an ingenious system for powering cranes and other machinery with hydraulics – was too small to handle heavy freight and larger ships. Its warehouses gradually became derelict, its trade was effectively wiped out during the severe winter of 1962-3 (when the Regent's Canal froze), and it closed to commercial shipping in 1969. A striking description by Hugo Marchant tells us how it looked before the start of Docklands regeneration.

"When I first visited it in the early 1980s the basin, with its dilapidated wooden jetties and low rise warehouses, was eerily quiet in the way that only a formerly clamorous industrial site can become when abandoned. The railway to the north was disused and the road and river to the south had little traffic. Apart from a few gulls bobbing on the surface of the water there was little movement. Local fishermen spoke of a giant pike which had its home in the southwest corner of the silted up dock."[56]

Soon afterwards, ambitious plans for this locale were put in hand, and, from 1983, the Regent's Canal Dock began to be reborn as Limehouse Basin. There were further upheavals to come, notably the disruption caused by the construction of the Limehouse Link underground roadway in the early 1990s, but today's Basin, surrounded by smart properties and teeming with houseboats and pleasure craft, is agreeable and prosperous. That giant pike, though, must be long gone...and the place's turbulent previous existence is now preserved only in old photographs, and in the words of writers such as Thomas Burke.

> There are in Limehouse many sounds;
> A hundred different sounds by day and night.
>
> The crash and mutter of the dockside railway,
> The noise of quarrel, the noise of fist on face,
> [...]
> The noise of singers in the ships,
> Sounds of threat and sounds of fear...[57]

The DLR, which began operating here in 1987, is a polite, discreet shadow of the lumbering, steam driven goods trains Burke would have known. As it scurries prettily beside the Basin, it passes a curious relic of the Regent's Canal Dock: an octagonal, brick-built tower, festooned with ivy, and offering a fine potential vantage point for the Limehouse Curve. My initial speculations about its identity (Could it be some sort of Victorian folly? Or, with its distinctive chimney, a furnace, or a brewery?) were wrong, as I discovered when I explored the area on foot. In fact, it was a part of the old Dock's hydraulic power system – an 'accumulator tower', whose lower section once housed a cylinder in which water was compressed, with a gravel-filled piston, to 700 pounds per square inch, providing a consistent, high-pressure supply to drive the surrounding cranes, lock gates and other apparatus.

The Tower dates from 1869, and was one of the casualties of the Regent's Canal Dock's decline; prior to its refurbishment, the upper part of its chimney had vanished, and the building, "largely roofless and open to the elements,"[58] had initially been mistaken for a "railway lookout tower" by 1970s investigators.[59] Its restoration, funded by the London Docklands Development Corporation, was undertaken, in the mid-1990s, by Dransfield Owens de Silva, an architectural design firm whose other projects have included a number of London warehouse conversions. They installed a internal spiral staircase, added a viewing platform, and rebuilt the chimney to its former height.[60]

The Accumulator Tower used to be open for regular viewings, but has recently been closed to the public during the construction of new flats close by. We were fortunate to gain access to it despite this building work, and are grateful to the Canal River Trust and the Ardmore Group for making our visit possible; we'd like to say a special 'thank you' to Sheamus Tierney, Ardmore's Project Manager, who gave us every possible assistance while we were onsite. However, I must admit that I came away from the Tower with mixed feelings. Its revamp has been highly effective, but lovers of industrial archaeology, hoping to find a precise replica of a remarkable feat of Victorian engineering, will be disappointed. The new staircase – which certainly looks as though it's always been there - has inevitably ousted some of the accumulator's components, and the fine woodwork captured in our photographs would have had no place or function in the original, dusty, noisy installation.

But how good it was to gaze down at the DLR, and the start of the Curve, from the Tower's platform; or to peer at them through its ivy-clad window! From a moving train carriage, only a confusing glimpse of the old bridge is possible: up here, the scene had the intricate clarity of a model railway layout, and there was a telling visual contrast between the operational DLR (its trains in their smart, predominantly red livery, its trackside railings in immaculate blue) and the Curve, clad in its own, forlorn colours, and overrun with bristling weeds.

It's only a short distance from the bridge to the now-vanished Salmon Lane junction, and the Tower would have given 19th century spectators - had they found a way to climb it - a bird's-eye view of incidents such as the collision there in January 1883, when a goods service from Millwall Junction, taking the Curve en route to Stratford, "ran into a workmen's train which was running from Barking to Fenchurch Street."[61] Major injuries were avoided only because the engine of the goods train struck an unoccupied carriage, but both lines remained blocked for some time.

Today, we can't see beyond the solid wall confronting the bridge in Lowell Street - or follow the trails of the locos and trucks that would once have passed along here. We can only daydream about them and their cargoes - Kipling's "beef, pork, and mutton, eggs, apples, and cheese"; the "sugar, rum, molasses, coffee, or logwood" mentioned in Joseph Conrad's *The Mirror of the Sea*;[62] and, of course, Fyffes' bananas from East India Dock. I wonder whether the residents of the flats here ever catch phantom whistles and rumbles from the long-departed trains, or sense the presence of spectral bunches of fruit ("one banana, two banana...") in their shiny new kitchens?

The northern end of the Curve, its path blocked by the flats on the right

Looking south; the DLR (left), the Accumulator Tower, and the Curve

An easterly view from the Tower, showing the Curve's junction with the main line (now the DLR)

The start of the Curve from the other direction

Inside the restored Accumulator Tower; its finely decorated roof and spiral staircase

This staircase leads down into the Tunnel approach from Butcher Row

PEDESTRIANS IN THE ROTHERHITHE TUNNEL

A bridge or a viaduct permanently changes an area's topography; and the gouges of a railway cutting, though lower-lying and more shadowy, are equally indelible. But river tunnels make far less visual impact upon their surroundings: those that are actually completed reveal themselves only where they surface; while the many aborted ones collapse and are usually washed away, leaving no physical traces at all.

One such failed, vanished project was an "Archway or Tunnel" for carriages and pedestrians beneath the Thames between Rotherhithe and Wapping, authorised by Act of Parliament in July 1805. It was praised at the time for its "singularity, novelty and boldness,"[63] and "engineers of the highest reputation",[64] including the Cornish mining expert and steam engine pioneer Richard Trevithick, were involved in its construction; but quicksand in the riverbed was a constant, potentially lethal problem for them, and after their south-to-north pilot tunnel, which had almost reached the Wapping side, was flooded twice in early 1808, work was suspended and eventually abandoned.

Marc Isambard Brunel's Rotherhithe-to-Wapping Thames Tunnel opened in 1843. Costly to build and never used for road traffic as intended, it has carried trains under the river since the 1860s. The Blackwall Tunnel (1897) and the Greenwich Foot Tunnel (1902) provided much-needed additional crossings, and in 1900, an Act of Parliament sanctioned a new subaqueous road and pedestrian route connecting Limehouse and Rotherhithe. Work began on it in 1904, and the *London Daily News* predicted that it would "bring prosperity to two ancient neighbourhoods, once the birthplace of heroes, but now only thought of as hopeless slums."[65] Its two excavation crews approached each other from opposite shores of the Thames, and, on 27 September 1906, were able to "[shake] hands through a hole made in the intervening wall of soil" at "what was practically the middle of the tunnel."[66] They finished their job in 1908, well ahead of schedule and without any major mishap,[67] but their achievements won fewer public plaudits than the completion of the Blackwall Tunnel 11 years earlier – perhaps because, as one newspaper put it, "the principles of under-river tunnelling which were largely experimental at Blackwall, have since become well established."[68] There were also protests over the thousands of homes demolished to make way for the new tunnel, and complaints that its approaches were "to be left unfinished, eyesores to every passer-by."[69]

The Rotherhithe Tunnel was some 4,860 feet long,[70] and, in the proud words of one of its engineers, "greatly facilitated road traffic between the Eastern and South-Eastern Districts of London."[71] It attracted international attention, and was inspected, in September 1908, by a 20-strong delegation from Leipzig, on an official visit to the London County Council which also took in Vauxhall Bridge, "the electricity generating station at Greenwich, [and] several housing estates."[72] As traffic steadily increased along its underground roadway, so, inevitably, did the number of accidents; in January 1914, it was reported that a cyclist had been crushed to death by being "thrown under the wheels of a motor-trolley trailer, when endeavouring to pass between it and the kerb."[73] Such incidents are sadly similar to more recent ones in the capital – but modern Londoners, accustomed to the Tunnel merely as a speedy route under the river for cars and lorries, may be surprised by accounts of extensive pedestrian use during its first, less polluted decades. The description below, published in 1909, conveys the excitement, shock, even wonder that would have been experienced by an early foot-passenger, and is worth quoting at length.

"As he approaches the top of one of the river-bank shafts he becomes aware of a rumbling noise, which gradually increases to a roar, like that of some great subterranean waterfall. Entering the dome covering the shaft he sees, far below him, lorries, cabs, omnibuses, and other vehicles, which emerge in turn from the tunnel, add their quota to the general din, and disappear again.

A spiral staircase leads him down many feet into the depths. Far away in both directions stretch the gleaming triple rows of incandescent electric bulbs, which, thanks to the white glazed tiles lining the tunnel, give a very satisfactory general illumination. Inspired with the wish to walk under a river, he starts off through the echoing tunnel towards the farther shaft. Noises spring into being suddenly, and involuntarily he turns his head, expecting to see a vehicle close behind him, and is surprised to find that the nearest is a hundred yards away. Owing to the peculiar resonance of the tunnel, it is hard to locate the cause of a noise by the ear with the accuracy possible in the upper world.

After quite a long tramp the distant shaft is reached, and many stairs have to be mounted. Presently the visitor emerges through a door-way, and finds himself overlooking wharves, where derricks are slinging cargoes into the holds of barges and small vessels. Looking back across the river, he is surprised to find how near the opposite bank seems to be - only a couple of stone-throws away."[74]

(The "river-bank shaft" mentioned at the start of the quotation is housed within a red-brick rotunda in what is now King Edward VII Memorial Park, on the north side of the river. From here, a long-disused spiral staircase leads down to the Tunnel; the pedestrian would have climbed the matching stairway on the Rotherhithe side, before exiting from a similar rotunda.)

Our visitor seems willing to put up with disorientation and ever-present, confusing noise as a trade-off for the novel experience of 'walking under a river.'

But his sensations are also disquieting ones - triggers for alarm, even panic - and the Tunnel was soon to gain a reputation as a strange place, associated with mysterious, secret, even violent events.

Dockers or sailors often fought there. In an extraordinary court case from July 1913, two Scandinavian seafarers – one of whom spoke only Finnish, the other only Swedish – were accused of taking part in an underground affray between seven men who had been "all on top of each other and all fighting with knives." Judicial proceedings were complicated by the fact that the man bringing the prosecution spoke only German: "the evidence had, therefore, to be translated in three different tongues."[75] Another case resulted from a fatal assault upon a strikebreaker during the General Strike of 1926. The victim, a 58-year-old man who had been working at a wharf near the Regent's Canal in Limehouse, was walking home towards Rotherhithe through the Tunnel "when a gang of five or six men attacked [him] from behind."[76] He received severe head injuries after being "felled with a heavy weapon",[77] and died in hospital. A striking docker was later convicted of his manslaughter.

Like other discreet London locations, the Tunnel was a "transient niche of privacy"[78] for sexual encounters, including liaisons between gay men; and the loneliness and desolation of its dark corners are poignantly communicated by a press report from December 1934 recording the discovery of an abandoned baby girl ("the middle toes on both her feet are abnormally long") at the top of one of its spiral staircases. The child had been found several weeks previously, and was "awaiting identification at the London County Council Institution [at] East Dulwich."[79]

According to census figures, traffic through the Tunnel in a sample 12-hour period almost doubled between 1927 and 1933,[80] while a report published in 1930 by the London Country Council stated that carbon monoxide levels within its confines were rising dramatically.[81] The underground route was clearly not somewhere to dawdle – and occurrences like the one in May 1931, when flames leapt out of the backfiring exhaust of an omnibus that was passing through, starting a fire that filled the confined space with "fumes and choking smoke",[82] must have further deterred pedestrian users. The spiral staircases, positioned well inside the Tunnel, were a convenient short-cut, making it unnecessary to walk its full length via the road entrances/exits, but air-raid damage led to their closure during World War II, and they have never been re-opened – increasing walkers' exposure to noise and exhaust fumes. It is scarcely surprising that foot traffic has declined markedly since the 1940s.

I first ventured inside in the late 90s. I'd intended to take what was then the Tube from Rotherhithe, but found the station unexpectedly closed, and couldn't be bothered to seek out alternative routes across the Thames. "Why not?" I thought idly, as the nearby southern entrance to the Tunnel yawned at me, and then inhaled me. (Both portals reek of burnt petrol and stale dust, especially in warm weather, but I wasn't deterred by the halitosis.) My careless mood didn't last long. It was early afternoon, and though the traffic was light, its threatening boom contributed to a growing sense of unease. Was I trespassing? I hadn't seen a 'keep out' sign, but there were no other pedestrians, and I began to notice that motorists were slowing as they passed, eyeing me up with derisive curiosity. I shut them out and kept walking, faster than usual.

Years afterwards, I read Iain Sinclair's powerful portrayal of the Tunnel in *Downriver*.[83] His references to "mean-faced" drivers and "white abattoir walls" are spot on, but I never experienced the degree of horror he describes when I was inside. My discomforts were bearable because, unlike truly Hellish ones, they had limits – end points defined by the numbers on successive signs beside the roadway, tallying the yards I'd already covered, and the diminishing number of those to come. They indicated that I was making progress; that if I didn't succumb to the fumes, or fall under a car or lorry, I could be sure of reaching the other side. And when I did get there, the sight of daylight was sweet; likewise the sonic segue from the grim din of the engines to the hesitant birdsong and throaty river noises of Limehouse. Talking of throats (ears and noses too), the Tunnel left me with a rasping, waxy, snotty memento of itself that lasted several days, and discouraged me from returning to what Sinclair calls "the worst London can offer" until work on this book gave me a pressing need to.

***

I'd often gazed down on the Tunnel's northern portal from the westbound platform at Limehouse DLR station, which gives a grandstand view of the vehicles rushing or inching towards it (via the 'bottleneck' restricting entry to anything wider than 6 feet 6 inches), and of the heavy gates that can swiftly close it off. Another good vantage point is the footbridge, accessible up a steep gradient from Horseferry Road, that carries the CS3 cycle route over the Tunnel approach and towards St. James' Gardens. From here, I'd spotted a way to avoid a long, dreary walk into the Tunnel: the staircases carved into each side of its mouth, leading down from the nearest main road, Butcher Row.

I'd passed the original northern pedestrian entrance, the riverside rotunda in King Edward VII Memorial Park, without realising what it was; and had also failed to notice its southern twin while looking across from the Wapping shore. Neither rotunda can be entered: the southern one is fenced off, and though the other stands in open ground, its doors and windows seem impenetrable.

I was looking forward to a more detailed exploration of the Tunnel itself – once I'd assembled some safety items. Anyone doing a photoshoot on a narrow pavement in a gloomy, fume-filled passage needs high-visibility vests and face masks: I acquired ours at the Screwfix store conveniently located on The Highway near the Limehouse Link, and we put them on at a bench in St. James' Gardens before walking round into Butcher Row, and making our descent.

Some things had changed since my last visit to the Tunnel. The traffic was heavier, though there were occasional lulls; and the reverberant noise was several decibels more intense than I remembered, making conversation difficult. Drivers and their passengers seemed uninterested in us (no slowing or gawping), and we encountered a couple of cyclists and a lone pedestrian, kitted out, as we were, in masks and hi-vis clothing. But there was the same feeling I'd had before − that, as walkers, we were irrelevant intrusions, barely tolerated on a major arterial route, and here very much at our own risk. The sense of imminent danger grew when we needed to cross the road, and had to dash for the opposite pavement in front of vehicles that seemed to have little intention of slowing down. Did they even notice us in their headlights?

The speeding traffic also paid no attention to the base of the northern spiral staircase, set back from the pavement, and grimy but well preserved. Its metalwork and surrounding tiles weren't caught directly by the ceiling lights, so their dark, matt surfaces contrasted with the wet-looking, public lavatory gleam of the main tunnel walls. The staircase was like a refuge; and as we climbed its lowest section (leading up to the rotunda in King Edward VII Memorial Park, but now sealed at roof level), and examined the bannisters and the still-legible surrounding signage, we were almost invisible to passing cars − even if they'd wanted to look at us.

We'd quite literally stepped aside from the main business of the modern Tunnel, and were able to relish this still-accessible part of the northern stairs for a few comparatively still, peaceful minutes, before re-connecting with the speed and hubbub of the roadway, and heading back to the Limehouse entrance. The experience had been fascinating − but I was reminded of the Tunnel's toxic slipstream ("In Limehouse, no one can hear you cough") when I inspected my face mask before discarding it. It was stained like the filter on a stubbed-out cigarette.

The two remaining ports-of-call on our Rotherhithe Tunnel agenda were the rotundas on either bank of the river. I wasn't sure how much they'd tell us, and was disappointed that we couldn't get close to the southern one, whose now-tranquil riverside surroundings would have been a shock to the pedestrians that once used it. The northern rotunda seemed more promising. It's largely unnoticed by passers-by (except circling runners and cyclists), but has been carefully tended - its brickwork vivid in the sunlight, and the plaque erected in 1922 to commemorate the 'navigators who, in the latter half of the sixteenth century, set sail from this reach of the river...to explore the Northern seas' clean and colourful. It has also been effectively secured against vandals, trespassers, and the merely curious who wish to see inside. However, with the aid of some wily photography, we were able to peer in and catch some tantalising glimpses of its interior.

I knew that behind the doors and the window grilles was the deep, metal-fenced stairwell that still serves as a ventilation shaft for the Tunnel. I could see little or nothing of it by squinting through the cracks in the doorframe, but what the camera captured was much more revealing, and far eerier than the clearer pictures of the underground part of the stairs. Were its curious results simply a consequence of faint light and restricted angles? Or were they a kind of concentration: a sample - filtered through a narrow gap like drawn-off vapour in a laboratory experiment, and somehow bottled by the photographic process - of an ambience that's been largely undisturbed for decades? I don't know, but later, as I gazed at the photos, they helped to paint other pictures in my mind: images of the succession of East Enders who'd once trodden those stairs; of that abandoned infant concealed in the shadows; and of the furtive things, sexual and criminal, that must have taken place there. But perhaps the play of illumination and gloom was reassuring, too. As my thoughts ran adrift, I recalled some words from Thomas Burke, the writer probably most closely associated with this part of London. They come from his *Song Book of Quong Lee of Limehouse*, published in 1920, and seem oddly, even perversely applicable to the atmosphere within the rotunda.

> My life is a great skirt of darkness,
> But human kindliness has torn it through,
> So that it shows ten thousand gaping rents
> Where the light comes in.

The Tunnel's walls, pavement and roadway, looking towards Limehouse. The trails of red light are from cars that have already vanished around the corner

The blocked-off staircase that connected the tunnel to the northern rotunda…

…and the rotunda itself, in Limehouse's King Edward VII Memorial Park

On the Rotherhithe side of the river: the fenced-off southern rotunda is in the foreground, while its northern twin can be seen in the distance, across the water

Glimpses inside the northern rotunda

This photo, looking north into Millwall Park, reveals the top of the viaduct, and its railway remnants. It was taken from an upper floor of a building in Manchester Road

MILLWALL: 'DESOLATION-LAND'

The earliest street map of London on my shelf was "drawn and engraved from authentic documents and personal observation" by B.R. Davies of Euston Square, and published in 1843. Its scale is 3¼ inches to a mile, and it shows the central part of the capital with impressive clarity. Eastern and south-eastern districts, though, look barer, and much of the Isle of Dogs (where, in the words of a famous seventeenth-century survey of Britain, the river "fetcheth almost a round compasse with a great winding reach"[84]) is almost blank. There are some helpful pointers, however: Davies notes that the area has "marshy ground, 7 feet below high water mark"; and the map provides a little more detail when representing the western shoreline beside Limehouse Reach, marked 'Mill Wall.'

For hundreds of years, there were actual windmills here: the 'wall' on which they stood was "a kind of earthen embankment",[85] buttressed with wood, and further reinforced against flooding with chalk, and later with ragstone.[86] In the nineteenth century, as the peninsula was industrialised, steam engines replaced the windmills, and "new factories sprang up along the wall, which was strengthened and straightened at the river's edge to allow ships and barges to be unloaded."[87] Millwall Docks (covering a total of about 200 acres, with 36 acres of water) began operating in 1868, and in December 1871, the single-track 'Millwall Extension Railway' connected them with the London & Blackwall line. The MER's final section - south from Millwall Docks, and then southeast via a brick viaduct to a station confusingly named 'North Greenwich' - opened in July 1872. (The current North Greenwich Jubilee Line station is on the other side of the river, near the O2.)

Perhaps the MER called its station 'North Greenwich' because of the nearby steam ferry which ran across the Thames to Greenwich Pier - or maybe the railway's proprietors were simply eager to avoid the unsavoury connotations of the words 'Isle of Dogs.' There was no shortage of disparaging printed comments about the place. In 1867, Thomas Wright wrote about its "slushy, ill-formed roads...tumble-down buildings [and] stagnant ditches";[88] fourteen years earlier, *Household Words* (a weekly magazine edited by Charles Dickens) had described it as a "mythical isle [with] very much the character of a *terra incognita*;"[89] and in 1905, an article in the *Strand* magazine by George R. Sims vividly portrayed the "Desolation-Land" at its centre. "All round the open space is a black fringe of grim wharves and of towering chimneys, belching volumes of smoke into a lowering sky that seems to have absorbed a good deal of the industrial atmosphere. This waste land is spanned by the soot-dripping arches of the railway, which is the one note of hope in the depressing picture, for occasionally a train dashes shrieking by towards a brighter bourne."[90]

Sims may have had an optimistic view of the railway, but there are stories of petty crime and tragedy associated with its southern end. The temptation to trespass on the tracks and have hazardous fun with rolling stock was clearly too great for a 13-year-old named Albert Lines, who, in 1887, was caught uncoupling goods wagons, opening their doors, and "pushing the trucks about" at a siding near North Greenwich station, assisted by some other youths who seem to have got away. The magistrate hearing the case was told that Lines had acted "merely out of mischief," but the boy had been in trouble before, and received ten strokes of the birch.[91] Two years later, the terminus was the scene of a more distressing event: the sudden death, on Christmas Eve 1889, of a middle-aged smith, Charles White, who "for the past two years had scarcely been sober." He suffered from *delirium tremens*, and, the night before he died, had been "rav[ing] about all kinds of animals, which he said were in [his] room." He spent the next day at work, and, that evening, was seen, looking "very strange", in a local pub by a colleague. White was given an egg beaten up in port (he had asked for whisky), and a group of concerned onlookers, including his brother-in-law, tried to help him home. Halfway there, the ailing man "could go no further, so they procured a barrow and wheeled him to the station, but when assisting him down the steps he expired." At his inquest, "the jury returned a verdict of death from alcoholic poisoning."[92]

The blighted conditions around the viaduct leading to North Greenwich were largely due to the nature of the surrounding terrain: former pasture, with soft soil that drained badly, and was unsuitable for building.[93] A useful purpose was finally found for it in 1901, when Millwall Athletic Football Club adopted it as their football ground. They stayed until 1910, and their presence put this one-time wasteland, quite literally, 'on the map' - where, in fact, the outline of the Millwall pitch lingered for several more years, marked 'disused.' Its site was purchased, in 1919, by London County Council, which began to develop it, and the neighbouring area, as Millwall Recreation Ground (now Millwall Park).

Viaduct and park had mixed fortunes in the following years. Passenger traffic on the railway, always light, was reduced further by World War I cutbacks. The London & North Eastern took control of the Millwall Extension in 1923, and closed down the North Greenwich terminus – which was subsequently demolished - three years afterwards. Services actually ceased a few weeks earlier than intended, when railway staff refused to cross dockers' picket lines during the General Strike in May 1926.[94] Though the Millwall line continued to serve the docks until the 1960s, it never ran on the viaduct again. The Recreation Ground, meanwhile, gained an open-air swimming pool in 1925, but the facility suffered irreparable bomb damage in the Blitz. Later in World War II, some of the adjoining land was converted to allotments as part of the 'Dig for Victory' campaign. These, and the ruins of the pool, are long gone, but the Park's grass, pathways and playgrounds remain, in the words of one local historian, "a popular place for relaxation, sport and other activities."[95]

***

When we were planning the shoots for this book, Olivia mentioned that she'd gone to meet a friend at Docklands' London City Airport in its early days, around 1990. She'd intended to walk there from the nearest bus stop, but recalled that the driver of her double-decker had been worried about her having to make her way through the "insalubrious" streets, and had taken her directly to the terminal, even though it wasn't on his route. She was grateful for his consideration, but added, "Wish I'd taken my camera to capture things as they were back then!" I have similar feelings about my lack of attention to the birth of the Docklands Light Railway. During the 1980s, it was establishing itself quite close to where I was living, but I rarely rode on the revolutionary new trains, and am especially sorry that I never visited the first, 'high-level' Island Gardens station, which was in service from 1987 to 1999.

Its track was carried on the old Millwall Extension viaduct – which had been disused for decades - across the Park as far as Manchester Road, then via a new bridge into what was, at the time, the DLR terminus. Construction work on the line had progressed smoothly, and the Greater London Industrial Archaeology Society reported in August 1986 that the viaduct itself had needed "only minor strengthening, some repair work and new parapet handrails."[96] A few months later, though, an alarming accident at Island Gardens stirred up safety worries. It occurred on the evening of March 10th 1987, when a normally 'automatic' test train being driven manually overshot the platform, ran through the flimsy buffers, and, in the words of London's *Evening News*, "was left hanging 20 feet in the air." Three staff members escaped unhurt, but the paper printed an embarrassing photograph of the damage, as well as some understandable (if unfair) expressions of concern from a local resident: "This must raise a lot of questions...Every railway station you see has colossal buffers. But up there, the station has just three bits of angle iron holding three red lights. That wouldn't even stop a BMX bike, let alone a runaway train."[97]

The incident, of course, was a one-off that couldn't have occurred with the automated systems in use; and changes to the path of the DLR at Island Gardens eventually made the prospect of runaway trains falling from the tracks an impossibility. When the line was extended across the river to Greenwich and Lewisham in 1999, the elevated Island Gardens station was replaced by the present, underground one, and the old viaduct retired once again.

After reading about the history of Millwall Park and the railway that once ran across it, it was time to remedy my lack of direct knowledge with a series of visits – first in winter, and, later, on several warm summer days. I took an immediate liking to this surprisingly extensive open space. On its skyline, instead of the "fringe of grim wharves and of towering chimneys" referred to by George Sims in 1905, is an intriguing, even bewitching view of the towers and tall cranes of Canary Wharf and the still-rising buildings to its east. From this distance, they look hazy and magical, putting me in mind (as Docklands often does) of the fantastic urban landscapes created by J.P. Martin and his illustrator, Quentin Blake, in the 'Uncle' books I first read as a child. Uncle, a benevolent, autocratic elephant, "lives in a house called Homeward, which is hard to describe, but try to think of about a hundred skyscrapers all joined together...and you'll get some idea of it. The towers are of many colours...[with] switchback railways running from tower to tower..."[98] (Those switchbacks are especially reminiscent of the DLR, with its ability to negotiate bends and steep gradients impossible for conventional, heavier carriages.)

The old viaduct, created for a more regular kind of railway, is a constant presence here; but it doesn't dominate or impose itself to the same extent as its cousins at Shoreditch or in Pinchin Street. This is partly because it's less massive, and is in better condition; but as I looked at it from a distance, and then close-to, I had the impression that it wasn't merely a relic, but an active participant in the current life of the Park. At one end, cricket nets have been set up within it; Millwall Rugby Club has been based at the other end since 2009, and its team use the Park for matches. And the unoccupied central section is certainly a beguiling spot for photography, and what I might seek to glorify as 'serious' exploration...though I suspect that as I weaved in and out of its arches, I was having just as much fun as the kids on the nearby slides and swings. I even found myself picturing the viaduct as a benign, sleeping giant, happy to fulfil the changing needs of successive generations of local residents, and to play whatever part might be demanded of it: railway bed, haven for sports lovers, subject for artists and photographers – or simply a place for hide-and-seek, a wall to lean against, and a shelter from rain and sun.

The viaduct at ground level, in the Park and (bottom left) from Manchester Road. The photo on the
bottom right shows its elegantly symmetrical internal arches

The 'ski-jump' at the end of the EGGS Bridge

A VIEW FROM THE EGGS BRIDGE

'Docklands' is a seductive word. It represents not just a location, but something of a lifestyle choice for many of the Londoners who live and work there. It's bound up with heady notions like *regeneration*, *extension*, and *connection*. And it's hard to find the right collective noun for the innumerable projects proposed for the place by a succession of schemers. Maybe we should choose one of the three alternatives suggested (in relation to Australian urban planning) by Raymond Bunker: "plenitude, plethora or plague."[99]

The endless brochures, pamphlets and websites setting out 'visions' for Docklands can read like utopian catalogues, full of undeniably praiseworthy concepts: *new initiatives*; *harmonious transformations*; *fast-track redevelopments*.[100] But a substantial proportion never come about. Policies change; money runs short; local opposition intervenes...and a percentage of the proposals are quietly binned. The documents associated with them still survive, though - a sad flotsam of inflated language, broken hyperlinks and dead email addresses, washed up, years or even decades later, by internet searches. Filtering out such outdated, misleading stuff (not to mention the clouds of error and myth that are always present in cyberspace) when trying to establish the facts can be complicated – as I discovered while grappling with a conundrum relating to somewhere I once lived: Gallions Reach.

Just about within Docklands (it lies a little to the east of London City Airport), Gallions Reach has far more in common with neighbouring Beckton than with Canary Wharf or Blackwall. For a century, the Beckton area (I'd struggle to say where Beckton ends and 'Gallions' begins) was dominated by its Gas Works, which opened in 1870, and once supplied 45 million customers[101] "through gas mains that were four feet in diameter."[102] The 500-acre works closed in 1969, leaving ugly levels of pollution behind; as recently as 1994, "a doctor treating residents of an estate built [there] blamed an outbreak of migraines, skin rashes and diarrhoea on [the] contaminated soil."[103] Some of the site remains undeveloped, but over the last four decades, Gallions Reach, like Beckton itself, has evolved from grimy desolation to increasing prosperity.

Much of its fresh life has been brought in by new transport links, laid like arteries across what the old maps call the 'East Ham Level.' One of the most significant of them is Royal Docks Road, a part of the A1020 that was known, at the time of its opening on 3rd October 1989 by Department of the Environment Under Secretary Colin Moynihan, as the 'Eastern Gateway Access Road.' It heads north for about a mile from what's now called Gallions Roundabout to a junction with the A13 and the North Circular Road (A406), and was a key component of the London Docklands Development Corporation's 'Docklands Highways network' - an initiative intended to "open up the 720 acres of the Royal Docks as the major development opportunity for London from now [1989] into the [21st] century."[104]

Three months after the Access Road was inaugurated, work began on another project that was to transform this part of East London: the £280 million extension of the Docklands Light Railway east from Poplar via Canning Town, and along the northern edge of the Royal Victoria Dock towards an elevated station at Gallions Reach (close to the roundabout where the Access Road started), and on to a terminus at Beckton. The new line opened on 28th March 1994: the A1020 runs initially to its west, before the tracks pass beneath it en route to Beckton. Northeast of Gallions Reach station, the DLR's train maintenance depot occupies part of the old Gas Works site.

The Docklands Highways Network was an example of a successful strategy that "secured significant benefits for local residents;"[105] and the initially under-used DLR extension has also more than proved its worth. But as already mentioned, there are other bold plans that never got off the ground, or are still being debated. In the Gallions Reach area, the biggest unresolved scheme is the one for an additional Thames crossing. I'm not going to attempt to summarise its complex history here (any account would be out of date before it was published), but the prospect of a link across to Thamesmead appears to have influenced road-building policy around Gallions Reach, where some recently constructed thoroughfares seem wider than necessary, and may, perhaps, be elements of a future route to (and over) the river.

For some time, I ascribed the existence of a curious local 'white elephant' - the truncated road bridge over the A1020, just north of the station – to an abandoned river crossing scheme. I first caught sight of the structure from the platforms at Gallions Reach DLR, and its chopped-off absurdity so impressed me that I decided to seek out other 'going nowhere' places around the capital...and start work on this book. Finding out more about it, however, was a challenge. I discovered that its proper name was the 'Eastern Gateway Grade Separation'[106] (EGGS for short). The "right to construct and maintain a bridge over part of the railway line to the east of the Eastern Gateway Access Road" was one of a series of government proposals announced in February 1990;[107] and I unearthed an architect's drawing giving details of the bridge's design, and of some of the materials from which it was made: fair- and aggregate-finished concrete, red and white polished brickwork, and handsomely decorated steelwork for its lighting towers.[108] I couldn't obtain the date of its completion from the architects or from Newham Council, but it was almost certainly in place prior to the opening of the

Beckton DLR extension in March 1994.

My initial belief − echoed in a number of road devotees' blogs - that the EGGS bridge was part of the northern approach to an aborted river crossing seems to have been wrong. I found information about its true purpose buried in an LDDC press release, which states that a "link to [a] proposed shopping centre on the Albert Basin will pass over the Eastern Gateway Access Road."[109] (This must refer to the EGGS bridge, as there's no other route over the highway here.) The Basin lies east of the Royal Albert Dock, and to reach it, a slip road from the bridge across the A1020 would have had to run a few hundred yards southwards. But due to a change of policy, the shopping centre wasn't built there (Gallions Reach Shopping Park, opened in 2003, is sited well to the north, on former Gas Works land), and EGGS, which currently carries road traffic in only one direction - southbound from the A1020 onto the A117 towards Beckton station − never 'touched down' east of the railway lines.

Its dramatic mid-air termination inspired a local nickname, 'the ski-jump bridge', and in 1995, it was used for a memorable stunt in *Out of the Hive*, an episode of the BBC One television series *Bugs* ("*The Avengers* of the 90s") in which a burning car drives off it and explodes when it hits the ground. More recently, the secluded area near its western end has been widely used "for the fly-dumping of large quantities of commercial waste [and] burned out cars,"[110] as well as for legitimate parking. It's currently on the books of a film facilities company whose website describes it as "a fantastic controllable road...[and] a location for all your creative briefs including driving/car scenes looking for a cinematic backdrop."[111] Its photogenic qualities are undeniable − as our pictures demonstrate.

There's an odd postscript to my efforts to learn more about the 'ski-jump bridge.' It certainly *looks* substantial and purposeful enough to have been intended for some kind of grand scheme − and no doubt this is why so many people (myself included) believed it had been created as part of a new cross-river route. It probably wasn't: but in a strange twist of fate, it may have been considered recently for that very role. In October 2012, Transport for London published a consultation document on the topic of Thames river crossings: it discussed "connecting [a] Gallions Reach Ferry to the existing road network", and suggested that one means of doing so would be via "the partially complete bridge structure over the Royal Docks Road"![112]

The fenced-off top of the bridge; the slip road to the left connects to the A1020

The bridge's distinctive steel towers, seen from the roadside

The bridge, looking north at Gallions Reach. The remains of a gasometer are visible in the distance, and the blue-and-red buildings are part of the nearby DLR depot

The view from the other direction: the line towards Gallions Reach DLR station is on the right, and the curved track to the left leads into the depot

Looking west towards Ravenscourt Park station

BESIDE THE TRACKS IN HAMMERSMITH AND EAST PUTNEY

On a few occasions, our pleas for admittance to particularly hard-to-reach sites were politely turned down by their wary keepers. These refusals were disappointing, but understandable: owners and guardians are jealous of their privacy; exclusivity depends, by definition, on keeping most people out; and in some cases, granting access to isolated, hazardous spots – especially those with trains running nearby - may be impractical, too expensive, or just too plain risky.

It was almost certainly safety worries that led to the denial of our requests to visit a couple of London's most curious railway ruins: the remnants lying between and above the lines at Hammersmith and East Putney. The first of these locations is the more accessible – but even here, the prospect of getting from the open-air Tube tracks onto the brick viaduct east of Ravenscourt Park station is almost impossibly daunting for anyone without a cherry picker – or wings. Nevertheless, I'd always wanted a better look at this structure than the one available from the carriages of District and Piccadilly Line trains; and when we learned that we couldn't actually set foot on it, our search began for a vantage point from which to observe and photograph it.

The King's Mall multi-storey car park off Glenthorne Road was a possible candidate, but we were able to access a better one on the south side of the tracks, providing downward and westward views. From here, we could see the smartly painted green bridge, dating from 2010, that carries the lines over Cambridge Grove - its 80-year-old predecessor had been beyond repair, due to decades of rainwater damage[113] - as well as most of the old viaduct, which rises steadily from the west, nudging in between the tracks, and ends abruptly near the car park. Two footbridges cut across it like belligerent, outstretched arms: one connects the car park to the King's Mall Shopping Centre, but the other is out of use at the time of writing, its northern side gaping aimlessly in mid-air above a building site.

After setting aside my modern maps of the area, and delving back into the nineteenth century – when things looked very different - I found out that the viaduct had formed part of a line that belonged to the London & South Western Railway, but was generally known as the 'Kensington and Richmond.' This opened on New Year's Day 1869, after being inspected, a few days earlier, by "a special train, conveying a large number of professional gentlemen,"[114] including a representative of the Board of Trade. Its route was about six miles long, branching off from 'Richmond Junction' (just north of Addison Road station, which is now called Olympia) down to a vanished stop at Grove Road (now Hammersmith Grove). From there, it ran southwest, "cross[ing] the Grove by a very fine lattice bridge of 90 feet span",[115] then headed "nearly due west"[116] on the viaduct shown in our photos, whose western end was at the long-vanished Studland Road junction. Ravenscourt Park station hadn't yet been built (it dates from 1873, and was initially called 'Shaftesbury Road'), so the next stop on the line was Turnham Green. Beyond it, the line went towards Richmond, crossing the Thames via Strand-on-the-Green bridge.

Just prior to its launch, a journalist observed that the route "passes through a district not very extensively built upon, but which at no distant day will tempt many speculative builders."[117] Its presence certainly played a part in 'urbanising' the area: Hammersmith itself, to quote railway historian Christian Wolmar, had once been "a village...[long] known for its spinach and strawberries, but now had begun to assume its present-day reputation as a transport interchange, a place to pass through."[118] The new line attracted crime and vandalism, too. In May 1869, the Surrey Sessions court heard a case against Ephraim William Blackburn, "a respectable-looking lad" of 16, who had been "indicted for placing a large tin saucepan on [its] rails...thereby endangering the lives of passengers." Following his arrest, Blackburn had apparently tried to persuade the police to charge him merely with trespass, and had offered to pay a 40-shilling (£2) fine there and then. However, he was found guilty of "attempting to upset a railway train" (as a headline writer put it − vividly, if not in formal legal language), and sentenced to three months' imprisonment with hard labour.[119]

Two other companies, the Great Western and the Metropolitan, went on to operate trains to Richmond over the London & South Western's metals, but the path along the viaduct was to prove less convenient than the District Railway's newer line, which used the station on Hammersmith Broadway that's still in operation. District services began operating west from Hammersmith in 1877: they ran beside the viaduct, as they do today, connecting with the existing route to Richmond at the Studland Road junction. Passengers' preference for this more direct course destroyed the competitiveness of the Kensington and Richmond's. The last-ever trains to Grove Road ran on 3rd June 1916, and what Dan Waddell has described on Twitter as "the Hammersmith ghost viaduct, still standing, taunting the luxury flats [now] being built next to it,"[120] is virtually all that's left of what was once a pioneering train service.[121]

The LSWR, as well as establishing the route to Richmond via Turnham Green and Kew Gardens, also instigated another key component of the modern-day District: the line from Putney Bridge via East Putney, Southfields, and Wimbledon Park to Wimbledon. This "new railway" opened on 3rd June 1889; the week before, the *Pall Mall Gazette* had published a detailed account of it, penned by an anonymous journalist who was as excited as a train-spotting schoolboy to have "[made a] trial trip...on a contractor's engine", accompanied by two engineers. His article enthuses about the quality of the new stations and the fine bridge ("practically open[ing] up a new district") over the Thames, and contains a detailed description of a junction near East Putney where "the new line branches into two." One of the branches "runs forward, crosses the River Thames, and joins the District Railway at Putney Bridge station," while the other takes "a second but less direct route...to Waterloo."[122] To do so, it connects with the 'loop line', opened in 1846, that's shown in our two Putney photos. These look eastwards: out of sight around the corner lies Wandsworth Town, beyond which the line continues towards Clapham Junction and central London.

Constructing this connection required some substantial masonry, a good deal of which survives. Between the tracks stand massive pillars that once supported a 'flying junction' across the loop line, used by 'up' trains from Wimbledon to get onto the Waterloo-bound metals. The large viaduct on the right of the first picture runs roughly parallel to Oakhill Road (which lies to its south), and was for 'down' trains coming from Wandsworth Town and heading towards Wimbledon. The viaduct is still in use for stock movements – these now run in both directions - and to maintain drivers' route knowledge;[123] main line trains also run over the East Putney to Wimbledon line "during engineering works"[124] and at other times. The flying junction – described in a 'vignette' published in 1966 as a "high grassy single-track embankment"[125] - remained operational until the late 1980s, but according to a web posting by a former driver, it "fell into disuse [because it] was deemed unfit for the passage of trains", and its rails were lifted in early 1987.[126] The flying bridge itself seems to have been removed soon afterwards, leaving the pillars decapitated.

***

It's impossible not to be impressed by the sheer size of the railway ruins in this chapter: our failure to get as close to them as we'd wanted didn't really matter, as we could make out so much, even from a distance. Their massiveness is also a reminder of the amount of heavyweight civil engineering that's needed to construct flying junctions and viaducts for standard trains; the weaving, plunging trackways built for the Docklands Light Railway seem astonishingly flimsy in comparison. And although it's tempting to romanticise the structures in Hammersmith and Putney as lonely leftovers, they strike me as being different in character from those we saw at Limehouse, Pinchin Street and Bishopsgate. This is because they stand within (not beside or at one remove from) busy, functional railway sites, and must still - despite their verdant, unruly-looking foliage - be subject to the kind of routine inspections and maintenance undergone by other trackside components and artefacts. They clearly have their uses, too: the arches beneath the Hammersmith viaduct are convenient, dry places for storage, and some of them appear to have been secured with bars and grilles; and while it's very unlikely that the viaduct itself will ever carry trains again, there have been sporadic discussions, and proposals from MPs, about reinstating the flying junction at East Putney in order to provide more frequent services.[127]

The tracks cross Cambridge Grove on a steel and concrete bridge installed in 2010

The viaduct's eastern end, spanned by a footbridge. Beyond here, the lines turn towards Hammersmith

The dismantled flyover across the line towards Clapham, and its pillars in close-up

Cabling and fencing beside the tracks at Finchley Central

OUTER ZONE

AN INTERLUDE AT MILL HILL EAST

It's sometimes hard to make sense of London Underground junctions when observing them from a platform or a carriage window, but anyone taking the Northern Line to High Barnet can see the split at Finchley Central as clearly as in one of Frank Pick's classic maps. A 'breakaway' branch, less than a mile long, begins here: it runs, initially, alongside the main line, but quickly parts company with it, continuing to the northwest as Barnet trains turn north. The little line offers a glimpse of the expansive (and exclusive) greenery of Finchley Golf Club, but is stubbed out, almost immediately, at Mill Hill East - an old-fashioned, isolated stop that handles fewer passengers per annum than anywhere else on the system. In many years of Tube travel, I'd never visited it, but was sure it would make a suitable subject for this book.

The route made an odd impression on me. At first, I was simply irritated by it. I'd arrived at Finchley Central on a Barnet service just as a Mill Hill one was pulling out, and had to wait ten minutes for another. When I got into it, I thought we'd be on our way fairly swiftly, but further delays were in store. The handful of people in my carriage watched with curiosity, then disquiet, as a Transport for London staffer began lifting up the cushions on several unoccupied seats. After making a call on his mobile, he instructed us to move to another coach, and closed the doors on the one we'd vacated. Several more minutes went by, and with them, a number of trains to and from Barnet. Clearly, the Northern Line hadn't shut down, but I started to wonder whether, by crossing onto the Mill Hill-bound track, I'd broken away from the normalities of TfL (what its Tannoy announcements describe as 'a good service'), and shifted into some sort of parallel, 'Going Nowhere' sector. No special fares were payable here (we were still officially in Zone 4), but was our brief journey going to take us into a different domain - one where we could expect singular, even peculiar occurrences and experiences?

I found myself indulging in increasingly bizarre speculations about my surroundings. A jangling sound heralded the approach of a train driver (or jailer?) with a heavy keychain on her belt. Were we heading for lock-up when we reached our destination? The train's motor began whirring – a more hopeful sign – and just before the doors closed, a family party, each clutching a bulging sandwich and a drink with a straw, took their seats. Perhaps they knew something I didn't: should I, too, have laid in extra provisions?

As we finally left Finchley Central, I put a sock in these inanities, and looked out of the window instead. To the right was the Golf Club, with its imposing clubhouse (formerly Nether Court, the home of a Victorian industrialist); farther along, on the other side, a sizeable Waitrose. But my daft mood returned when I saw a giant fibre-glass duck, perched on top of a stack of scrap, just outside Mill Hill East. And as I alighted, I was confronted with a platform sign whose meaning I couldn't fathom, though it read like a powerful expletive: 'D OFF.'

My train, with the doors to one of its carriages still sealed, would shortly be heading back to Finchley Central; but I postponed my own return, as I wanted to check out the local sights. First on my list, inevitably, was the duck...but I was also eager to examine what lay beyond the station's buffers, and I walked round into Bittacy Road to do so. The edge of the station site was, of course, fenced off, but the tracks had once continued to the west here, though there was little more than a grassy embankment to show their path. The entire set-up at Mill Hill East was an enigma, and I suspected that the mockery I'd been indulging in was really a symptom of my bafflement with it. I clearly needed to find out more about this curious, underused corner of the network.

***

The line that once passed through Mill Hill East was part of the Edgware, Highgate and London Railway – and though the *Illustrated Times'* description of it, published in October 1867, is undoubtedly something of a puff piece (a suitable name for a laudatory article about steam trains?), it's hard not to be won over by its eager optimism. The EH&LR had opened on 22nd August that year. It ran from Seven Sisters Road (now Finsbury Park), northwest via Stroud Green and Crouch End to Highgate, on through Finchley to today's Mill Hill East (then known simply as Mill Hill), and thence towards its terminus: the "utterly rustic and sleepy village" of Edgware. The write-up rejoiced over the new line's superiority to the "'busses' [sic] and the 'carrier's cart'" that had been the previous means of transportation in some of these "remote and inaccessible region[s]". The railway had already brought "the benefits of...cheap and rapid communication [to] many thousands of passengers," and would doubtless lead to "the extension of building operations in the neighbourhood" - attracting, as new residents, "those sensible Londoners who prefer pure air, quietude, and rural beauty to the peculiar and semi-stifled existence which is called 'living' in the 'great metropolis.'"[128] In reality, according to a later commentator, its principal traffic was expected to be goods, and especially coal, "the passenger service being a secondary object in those early days."[129]

Constructing this nine-mile-long stretch of EH&LR had cost some £400,000. It was owned and run by the Great Northern, which went on to complete what is now the Northern Line to High Barnet in 1872: after the 'Grouping' of 1923, the

GNR became part of the London & North Eastern Railway (LNER). Mill Hill itself, in the early 1870s, was a village comprising about 190 houses, with a population of some 1,180.[130] It was surrounded by farmland, though the North Middlesex Gas Company opened a gasworks there in 1862; the railway, when it came, five years later, ran just to the north of the gas holders; nearby was a private siding, used for coal deliveries. The gasworks supplied "Finchley, Hendon, Mill Hill and a part of Golders Green":[131] it was run by the North Thames Gas Board from 1949, and survived into the 1970s. One of the buildings erected on the place where it stood is the Waitrose store visible from the train.

Another event that helped to transform Mill Hill from village to busy outer suburb was the development of the Inglis (or Mill Hill) Barracks. Built, in 1904, a little to the north of Mill Hill station ('Mill Hill East' from 1928), they were used first by the Middlesex Regiment and the Dalston Militia, and subsequently occupied by the Royal Electrical and Mechanical Engineers and several other corps and regiments. The barracks often earned a mention on the station's train tickets and in its timetables ('Mill Hill East for Mill Hill Barracks'), and their military significance was a convincing reason to press ahead with electrifying the Finchley-Mill Hill East spur in the face of World War II cutbacks. The conversion took place as part of a transfer to London Underground: on 12th April 1940, the *Hendon & Finchley Times* reported that "the last steam passenger train has run on the old London and North Eastern Railway between...Mill Hill and Finchley,"[132] and announced the temporary closure of the route, pending its switch to electric traction. In spite of wartime restrictions, this was accomplished in little more than a year, and Mill Hill East re-opened, as part of the Northern Line, on 18th May 1941.

London Transport's more ambitious plans, which had included the takeover and electrification of the entire Edgware, Highgate and London Railway, never came to fruition. There were no more Mill Hill East to Edgware passenger trains after September 1939, and freight haulage between the stations was handled by steam and diesel locomotives until the section's closure in 1964.

***

Trains once brought a steady flow of goods and people to and through Mill Hill East, but with the M1 and other major roads within easy reach, and no need for coal deliveries to the gasworks (itself rendered obsolete by the advent of natural gas), the railway here has undeniably declined in importance. Might it one day go the same way as some of the area's other former assets – such as the gasworks site (big enough to accommodate not only a supermarket, but a substantial number of houses and a gym); and the barracks, closed in 2007, and currently being "transformed into a high-quality new homes development" by Taylor Wimpey?[133]

There are precedents for selling off derelict stations and old tunnels elsewhere in the capital,[134] and a certain amount of redundant space around Mill Hill East - but the line (though its services were cut back in 2006) seems likely to survive, thanks in part to pressure from the Mill Hill Preservation Society and the London Assembly. The station, described by London railway expert Nick Catford as "one of the most basic on the underground network",[135] is not without its weird charm – and following my own easy and comparatively fast return journey (on a train driven by the same keychain-bearing TfL driver I'd encountered on my strange outward trip), I was able to decode the mysterious 'D OFF' sign I'd seen there. 'D' stands for 'de-icing equipment', and 'off' indicates, quite simply, that it's not to be used.

The parting of the ways beyond Finchley Central - Mill Hill East to the left, West Finchley and stations to High Barnet on the right

An abandoned fibre-glass duck rules the roost in this skip near Mill Hill East station

The buffers at Mill Hill East, seen from the platform, and (below) from near Bittancy Road

A disused signal, and a range of warnings and notices to train drivers, at the end of
Mill Hill East's platform

Where the M12 would have been…an uncompleted slip road beside the M11's southern carriageway. Roding Valley Park lies to the left

M12 – THE MOTORWAY THAT NEVER WAS

As an almost life-long Londoner, I sometimes feel a degree of unease when I leave the capital, although my stress levels are lowest when the exit is smooth and swift. Express trains north out of King's Cross accelerate so rapidly that I can barely read the names of the passing stations, but once I catch sight of Potters Bar, I know that the process of expulsion is over, and that it's time to start thinking about (and even looking forward to) my destination. Southerly departures, either by rail from Victoria or Waterloo, or down the A23, are also comparatively easy, if slower; while most of my trips to the west these days are by coach, and I always look forward to being sped away along the elevated A40.

Routes leading eastwards inspire more mixed emotions, due to childhood memories of taxing family journeys to Suffolk in the 1960s, and the battles through the rush hour to Caledonia Street coach station, near King's Cross, that preceded them. We were invariably late and overloaded with luggage on these expeditions; and our anxiety seemed to rub off onto those around us. On one occasion, as we headed for Caledonia Street at about 10 mph on a double-decker, I watched a fat, bespectacled commuter, his face flushed with exasperation and strain, running alongside with a briefcase in his hand, trying frantically to jump on board. "Blast you!", he shouted furiously at the bus, its conductor and its occupants as they drew away from him.

Having finally scrambled into the Suffolk-bound coach (operated by Jennings of Ashen, which had been serving this route since 1930), we'd edge into the heavy evening traffic and make our way towards Leytonstone. I was unfamiliar with the eastern suburbs back then, but I believe we followed the old A11 (now the A1199: Hollybush Hill), and passed the 18th-century High Stone that gave Leytonstone its name. Its now-faded mileage markings - *To Epping XI Miles through Woodford, Loughton; To Ongar XV Miles through Woodford Bridge, Chigwell, Abridge* - would have been known to generations of travellers. A little to the north, Hollybush Hill merges into Woodford Road; the once-leisurely traffic here was described in 1832 by Thomas Hood, who lived nearby:

> Along the Woodford Road there comes a noise
> Of wheels, and Mr. Rounding's neat postchaise
> Struggles along, drawn by a pair of bays,
> With Rev. Mr. Crow and six small Boys...[136]

Mr. Jennings' coach – the 60s' equivalent of Mr. Rounding's vehicle - would have continued along the old A11 (a former stagecoach route) to Woodford Green, and on through Epping Forest.

***

The Woodford area is an important conduit for traffic moving to and from the capital (or around its perimeter, via the North Circular Road), and words from Virginia Woolf's evocation of *1907* in her novel *The Years*, though not written for it, capture the murmuring expectation of its highways: "Even the horses, had they been blind, could have heard the hum of London in the distance."[137] But since the days of horse-drawn travel, the pressure and congestion on its roads have grown steadily – checked only by the shortages of World War II, during which fuel and tyre rubber were rationed, and services like Jennings' stopped short at Bishop's Stortford railway station in Essex, some 30 miles from the capital.[138] Petrol de-rationing in 1950 contributed to what the *Essex Newsman* called the "steady stream of cars [now] roaring through the otherwise quiet Essex streets";[139] and closer to London, there were frequent stories of hold-ups and bottlenecks. Prior to the completion of a £250,000 improvement scheme in 1957, Eastern Avenue (A12), "a road used by a vast volume of traffic travelling from east London, [used to] narrow to a single track" on a bridge over the Central Line at Newbury Park station;[140] and by the 1960s, both the North Circular and the Woodford High Road (the old A11, taken by the Jennings coach) "were carrying continuous streams of heavy traffic."[141]

Further improvements to Woodford's highways were clearly essential: the most substantial of these was the construction of the M11 motorway to Cambridge, which starts near Charlie Brown's Roundabout in South Woodford - a complex junction with the North Circular, the Southend Road, and the Chigwell Road. The motorway, completed by 1980, provided a more direct exit from London than the A11; the route of its first section, north-east through the Roding Valley, had been chosen in preference to a more easterly path via the Lea Valley.

Another motorway was planned in tandem with the M11. It began as one of the 'Radial Routes' proposed in the 1940s by architect and urban planner Sir Patrick Abercrombie, and received the designation 'M12' in 1969 - although for some time to come, official documents would continue to refer to it as 'Radial Route 7.' Originally, it had been intended "to act mainly as a by-pass to the existing A12, between the western end of the Brentwood by-pass and the Roding Valley", and would have been just less than 10 miles long.[142] By May 1972, a detailed 'Traffic Study and Economic Appraisal' had been undertaken for it: "24 ft wide connecting carriageways" would be needed to "join [the new road] to the outer slip roads of the M11" a little to the northeast of Charlie Brown's

Roundabout, and there would eventually be "dual three-lane carriageways of M12 between [them]."[143] Political opposition subsequently put paid to the project, and a later version of the M12 (starting in Roding Valley as before, but continuing beyond Brentwood to serve an airport at Maplin Sands in the Thames Estuary) was abandoned when plans for the airport were dropped. A final M12 scheme, which would have connected to the A414 near Chelmsford, was axed in the 1990s.[144]

***

The 'Pathetic Motorways' webpages are full of fascinating, obscure information, and it was on them that I saw a photograph of the stub of roadway described by the site's creator as "the only bit of M12 that was actually built."[145] Even with his guidance, though, actually locating this 'nowhere road' wasn't entirely straightforward. It is, of course, impossible to miss Charlie Brown's Roundabout, which writer and film-maker John Rogers has called "a knot of motorway flyovers with an enormous metal pylon rising in the centre – a Ballardian wet dream."[146] And a satellite image of the area seemed to reveal the 'dead end' I was seeking. But how to reach it on foot? (I'd figured that a drive-by on the M11 wouldn't be workable.) I was far from sure of my bearings as I turned off the A113 near Maybank Avenue in South Woodford. This and several other local road-names – Cowslip Lane, Rose Avenue, Mulberry Way – must have been inspired by the area's bucolic past, but there was nothing very pastoral about my path towards the Chigwell Road Reuse and Recycling Centre, which led over an undistinguished-looking stream choked with weeds. To my right I could see a sibling of John Rogers' pylon: an ugly, buzzing protrusion that nevertheless seemed to harmonise with the refuse lorries I was frequently jumping sideways to avoid. It took me a moment to realise that I'd just crossed the River Roding - lauded in 1622 by Michael Drayton as:

> ...[the] best-beloved Flood;
> Which from her Christall Fount, as to enlarge her fame,
> To many a Village lends her cleere and noble name.[147]

As recently as 1877, the Roding Valley was characterised as "undulating and well-wooded country";[148] it was also a significant source of archaeological finds, such as the "rude flint implements of primeval man" described in the *Gardeners' Chronicle* five years later.[149] (The same article mentions the discovery of fossilised mammoth bones in nearby Ilford.) A few hundred yards upstream, "little Roding" regains some of her rustic charm as she approaches Woodford Bridge; and as I looked beyond the Recycling Centre into what was signposted as 'Roding Valley Park', I saw that a patch of countryside still survives here. The Park is popular with dog-walkers, cyclists, and even mushroom hunters (we met one on our photo-shoot). However, it has been summed up in an online posting as a "very beautiful woodland area in a very odd place,"[150] and this part of it is dominated by the north- and southbound carriageways of the M11.

East of the recycling plant, a roughly paved road, partially blocked by bins, led beneath the northbound motorway and across open ground towards its southbound carriageway - where, just above me, I could see the fragment of the M12 that I'd read about. The uncompleted slip was separated from the M11 by a single white line, and formed a sort of lay-by, fenced off on its other side by the barrier I was peering over. It was wide enough to accommodate a broken-down vehicle or a police car, and its surface was intact and free of weeds, but it was unmistakably a marginal place, disdained by passing traffic; even the M11's roadsigns had turned their backs on it. It should have extended roughly northwards, but went nowhere...and around it, and near the thin trees beside the carriageway, was a remarkable variety of rubbish – not just tins and bottles, but larger items, even a decaying armchair. Evidently, 'anything would go' here (or almost anything: at least there were no burned out cars like those that had once been left near the ski-jump bridge in Gallions Reach[151]), and the cast-off debris formed an unsightly line of disjunction between the motorway and the pleasant surrounding greenery.

It took only a few minutes to check out this sad little spot, but I spent much longer looking for other physical traces of the M12, and reading about it online and at the National Archives in Kew, which holds most of the relevant documentation. I found memos, surveys and often puzzling maps; I learned that space had been set aside for the unbuilt motorway, and that the paved areas I'd walked along beneath the carriageways could have been intended as 'minor roads' connecting to it. But ultimately, my researches petered out like the piece of concrete I'd struggled to reach...and perhaps the reason for the blank I drew lies in the nature of the M12 itself. Unlike most of the other places featured in this book, it's a 'might-have-been' rather than a 'has-been' - a scheme (or a series of them) that never came to pass, and made barely any physical or measurable impact on London.

Above: "a remarkable variety of rubbish" beside the M11
Below: Roding Valley Park - an oasis of semi-rural peace, bordered by carriageways and electricity pylons

Beneath the northbound (above) and southbound M11

One of the pillars supporting the M11's southern carriageway has some valuable advice for the author…

A side-on view of the Crescent Wood Tunnel's northern portal

THE CRESCENT WOOD TUNNEL

A 'Great Exhibition of the Works of Industry of All Nations' was inaugurated, by Queen Victoria, in London's Hyde Park on 1st May 1851. The event lasted some five months, attracted over six million visitors, and displayed an extraordinary range of products, inventions and materials within a vast, specially designed iron and glass 'Crystal Palace.' The building was dismantled after the exhibition, but an enlarged version, re-assembled in spacious grounds near Sydenham, was opened (once again, by Queen Victoria) "under circumstances of the most imposing splendour"[152] on 10th June 1854. It became, for a while, what the Royal Institution of British Architects has termed "one of London's major venues for events and exhibitions."[153]

Train links with central London were crucial to its viability. Directors of the London, Brighton & South Coast Railway had been closely involved in the Palace's purchase and relocation, and their company began providing services to it, via the 'West End of London and Crystal Palace Railway,' on its opening day. These ran on existing LBSCR metals as far as Sydenham, then took a newly constructed section of track to the Crystal Palace terminus that's still in use today.

The prospect of lucrative visitor traffic also encouraged a rival firm, the London, Chatham and Dover, to build its 'Crystal Palace and South London Junction Railway' from Nunhead (on its route from Ludgate Hill), via stations at Honor Oak, Lordship Lane, and Upper Sydenham to a second Crystal Palace terminus - with better pedestrian access to the exhibition site than the LBSCR's. There were two tunnels: the 439-yard Paxton Tunnel, near the new Crystal Palace station; and the slightly shorter Crescent Wood Tunnel, whose southern portal adjoined the platforms at Upper Sydenham. In June 1863, London, Chatham and Dover shareholders were told that "the sinking of the shaft[s]" for both "was in rapid progress;"[154] and within a few weeks, "about 15 yards per month"[155] were being excavated. The new line was introduced on 1st August 1865, but the opening of Honor Oak and Lordship Lane stations was delayed by several months, and Upper Sydenham wasn't operational until 1st September 1884.[156]

The long-awaited station would, according to a press report, "be of great convenience to the inhabitants of that portion of [the area] which is being rapidly covered with substantial dwellings"[157] - but in fact, it failed to achieve its hoped-for commercial success. The entire route from Nunhead was something of a disappointment: it was never heavily used by commuters, and its *raison d'être*, the Crystal Palace itself, was in steady decline by the end of the nineteenth century.

Nevertheless, Upper Sydenham had its share of curious incidents, one of which may even have had significant legal implications. In September 1889, its stationmaster, Gustavus Farrall, was summoned by the police "for allowing a ferocious dog to be at large [and] unmuzzled" on the premises. A passenger had been attacked by the animal in the station's booking office; but Farrall's barrister contended that the accusation against his client had no legal merit, because the station "was not 'a public place' [as defined in the Police Act], and...the Metropolitan Police had no jurisdiction there." Surprisingly, the magistrate agreed, and dismissed the summons, though he refused to award costs to Farrall, on the grounds that "the man who had been bitten should receive some compensation."[158]

Something more alarming occurred in late 1905. A gentleman, en route from Crystal Palace to Upper Sydenham, was asked, by a young girl in his train compartment, to 'shut his door.' "Looking up," he wrote later to the *London Daily News*, "I saw that the further [door] in my compartment had apparently gone," (it had turned through 180 degrees, and was flush with the side of the carriage), and "on rising to close it, the girl in alarm begged me to be careful that I did not fall out. Warned, I grasped the back of the seat with one hand, while I endeavoured, without success, to close the door with the other." The girl came to his assistance, and they finally "got it to just as we reached Upper Sydenham station. [...] Had I not been warned...but acted on the impulse of the moment," the frightened traveller concluded, "unaware of the resistance I should encounter, I should in all probability have been thrown out on the line."[159] It's a mercy the courteous passenger came to no harm – but his story, if things had gone amiss, might have inspired a memorable Edwardian parlour ballad: *He Perished While Closing the Door...*

In 1916, wartime economies led to the shut-down of the entire Crystal Palace and South London Junction route; when it reopened in 1919, many of its passengers were military personnel heading to and from the Crystal Palace 'dispersal unit' handling their demobilisation. The CPSLJ's electrification was not completed until 1925 (by which time, it was part of the Southern), and the catastrophic fire that destroyed the Palace on 30th November 1936 – "flames, rising to a height of 300 feet, made a dazzling red glare in the sky"[160] - were a terminal, if not immediately fatal blow to the line's prospects. It closed temporarily from 1944 to 1946, but struggled on for another eight years prior to a permanent withdrawal of service on 20th September 1954, and its tracks and stations are gone.

***

Conventional railways have difficulties with gradients; and their tendency to run in valleys, cuttings and tunnels disguises their very existence from people on roads and paths above. Sometimes, with no track or bridge in view, the only indication of a train's presence is the sound it makes as it passes - and the route of a disused, silent line can therefore be even harder to trace, especially in the hills of southeast London. I found this out the hard way when searching for the southern portal of the Crescent Wood Tunnel, where Upper Sydenham station also stood. To reach it, I took the Overground to Sydenham, walked northwest up Kirkdale, and then west along Wells Park Road. After getting lost in Wells Park itself, I regained my bearings, and headed through a small gate a little further up the road. Beyond it lay a steep, muddy footpath down into wilder woodland...and then, quite suddenly, to the top of the tunnel. My slippery descent continued towards ground level, and I was soon gazing at the blocked-off portal from a patch of undergrowth close to where the station platforms would have been.

The size of the tunnel's mouth, and its contrast with the surrounding trees and greencry, made a dramatic impression. I'd previously seen a old photo of Upper Sydenham station, with a weary-looking London-bound train emerging from the portal: a typically nondescript suburban railway scene. But now, with no trace of the station remaining, the portal has acquired a solitary grandeur, emphasised by the fact that I was seeing it from the perspective of a groundling in an old-style auditorium, not from the elevation of a railway platform, which would have reduced its impact. Other, mixed-up theatrical thoughts occurred to me. The portal seemed irresistibly like a proscenium arch, but entrances and exits would surely be inhibited by its forbidding barrier ('DANGER KEEP OUT'); even the ghosts of former passengers, however accustomed to delays and cancellations, would have given up waiting for their non-existent trains by now. But as I stood there, I had the same feelings of expectancy as a playgoer, and these were suddenly gratified by a strange moment like a curtain-up: a brief, unexpected show put on by sunlight (catching the tunnel's crown and keystone) and sound (the birdsong, mingling with wind in the trees) that I was able to carry away as part of my sense of the place, as if I were a satisfied member of an audience.

I was eager to see the northern portal too, and wished I could have taken the obvious shortcut to it – through the tunnel. But instead, I had to climb back to where I'd come from, walk around Crescent Wood Road to a gate into Sydenham Hill Wood, and head down yet another steep, damp path through the trees. The tunnel mouth here is similar to its southern sister, but its fencing (at the time of my visit and our photographs) was shiny and new, with an access door that was clearly in regular use, and storage containers close by. All this is the work of the London Wildlife Trust, which has managed the Wood as a nature reserve since 1982, and has created a refuge within the tunnel for the local bat population. Public access to its interior is, inevitably, prohibited, but wildlife-loving visitors to the portal were given a treat in May 2016, when a colourful mural was unveiled on it. Created by street artist Louis Masai, it depicts the Brown Long-Eared Bat (*Plecotus auritus*), a species that lives and roosts here.[161]

Local animal and plant life, not Victorian brickwork, are the targets for the conservation that's taking place in Sydenham Hill Wood – but the once-redundant tunnel has benefitted too. Like the Millwall viaduct, it has found a new role: one that doesn't involve a metamorphosis, but simply a pleasingly practical exploitation of the durability built into it by its creators. I think those engineers and craftsmen would be surprised, but delighted at the outcome.

The southern portal, with the afternoon sunlight catching its keystone

On the pathway down to the northern portal. The rear of the tunnel's top wall (above its keystone) lies to the left of the fence

The barriers across the northern portal, and the access door behind them

The propellors of the de Havilland Heron that's on display outside Airport House,
Croydon Airport's former terminal building

CROYDON AIRPORT

Croydon Aerodrome, beside what is now the A23 (Purley Way), was created by combining two smaller airfields, Beddington and Waddon. In December 1919, it was chosen to replace Hounslow Heath as the official "air terminus of London," and the capital's 'customs port' for air traffic. Croydon's location had been considered preferable to its predecessor's: "being farther away from the river, [it was] much less liable to become fog-bound."[162] When it opened on 29th March 1920, it took over the daily flights to Paris previously handled by Hounslow.[163] Other international destinations available to its first passengers included Amsterdam, Rotterdam, and (from 1923) Berlin.

A newspaper report published in September 1920 paints a vivid picture of "the small but remarkably prosperous self-contained village" that had grown up around the Airport (as it soon came to be called). The site's "more or less solid-looking offices" were built "on the Army hut plan", and mostly "painted in the colours of the various aeroplane companies [based there], which like their machines and offices to match. The customs house, passport office, waiting-rooms, garage, and a very up-to-date restaurant complete the arrangements for passengers' comfort and convenience."[164] In fact, the facilities – and the means of handling outgoing and incoming planes – were basic and somewhat makeshift. For several years, the aerodrome was actually crossed by a road (Plough Lane). It marked the previous division between Croydon's two constituent airfields, and its presence led to awkward and potentially hazardous manoeuvring, as the *Illustrated London News* described in October 1920: "Machines from the Continent land at a point on one side of the road, where there is plenty of open space, and after depositing their passengers, 'taxi' to their hangars, which are situated on the other side of the road. On the section of the road which they have to cross, the hedges have been removed, and during their passage all vehicular and pedestrian traffic is held up by a policeman...and an official sentry."[165]

Despite such drawbacks, Croydon Airport generated initial levels of excitement and enthusiasm that may be surprising to jaded 21st-century air travellers. There were eager press reports of its growing passenger numbers (the first weekend of June 1921 saw twenty-six "air expresses" arriving and departing, with 102 people on board;[166] in the 12 months to 30th June 1923, 15,627 travellers flew in and out[167]), as well as a story about a well-heeled gentleman who had acquired "a personal aeroplane with a uniformed mechanic-chauffeur", and delighted in "dropp[ing] in [on] surprised friends in various parts of England."

("On occasions he has come to ground in fields near their houses, and walked in, leaving his man to look after the aeroplane."[168]) Best of all, perhaps, is the newspaper account of "a man who haunts an aerodrome." This Croydon resident – a distant cousin of Kenneth Grahame's Mr. Toad? – had "an insatiable passion for flying...He sits in the aerodrome hotel, and then suddenly decides he will fly to Wales. He has flown [there] half-a-dozen times in a fortnight.[...] Last week he saw a huge...ten-seater [plane, and] promptly ordered one," taking several thousand pounds in cash out of his pocket to do so.[169]

While flying remained an expensive, exclusive means of transport, Croydon was handling more and more international departures and arrivals, and urgently needed better buildings and equipment. Work started on their provision in 1926, and what was effectively a rebuilt airport was opened, by the wife of the Secretary of State for Air, on 2nd May 1928. The road across it had been removed – though a stub of Plough Lane remained, and is still in place today, near the B272 – and there was an impressive terminal building with a control tower, as well as a new hotel, additional hangars, and other improvements.[170] Croydon now looked glamorous, boasted state-of-the-art air traffic control, and was to enjoy a further decade of prosperity. Those flying in and out included royalty, heads of state, movie stars, sportsmen and other celebrities: crime novelist Agatha Christie particularly enjoyed plane travel, and in *Death in the Clouds* (1935), her Belgian detective, Hercule Poirot, witnesses a murder while en route from Paris to Croydon; he shares his flight with (among others) a doctor, a dentist, a couple of archaeologists...and a writer of crime fiction.

There were soon to be other, darker reasons for the growing number of passengers coming into Croydon. The Airport Society's website records that "the run up to the Second World War saw a massive increase in...numbers as British holidaymakers rushed to return from Europe";[171] and in late March 1939, according to the *Daily Express*, "nearly 400 Jewish refugees streamed into Croydon in a succession of air liners - the biggest influx the airport had ever experienced. They came from Danzig, the Polish Corridor, Cologne, Berlin, Vienna, Switzerland - all over Europe." Not all were allowed to stay in Britain, and there were distressing scenes as those refused entry "had to be dragged out of the hall onto the tarmac. One man was carried into [a] plane."[172] When war was declared a few months later, Croydon's civilian flights ceased, and it became an important RAF base, suffering severe damage during the Battle of Britain. A memorial "to all connected with Croydon and its aerodrome who gave their lives either in the air or on the ground during the Second World War" was unveiled in 1991, and can be seen in our photos.

Croydon Airport returned to full civilian operation in February 1946, but its post-war future was immediately under threat. It couldn't accommodate the larger airliners now being introduced, and had no scope for expansion. A *Daily Mail* article, widely reprinted in the provincial British press, characterised its "dreariness" as "something to be avoided", adding that "in the past there has been too great a tendency to give every attention to the passenger while he is in the air, but to neglect him utterly when he is on the ground."[173] Heathrow (which was in operation by May 1946, and carried 60,000 passengers during its first year),[174] and Gatwick (which was nominated as London's second airport in 1950, and underwent an extensive expansion a few years later) were now starting a new chapter in British air travel – one that Croydon was to be written out of, despite the support it continued to receive both in Parliament and elsewhere. From May 1947, it "cease[d]...to rank as a civil airport except for the use of chartered planes",[175] but its fate was only sealed after what its local MP, Sir Richard Thompson, later called "a very long and protracted wrangle."[176] It handled its final scheduled departure on 30th September 1959.

***

People taking flights from Croydon during its 1930s heyday would mostly have arrived by car – probably in a taxi or a limousine. Day-trippers, visiting it in order to absorb the still-unfamiliar ambience of aviation, would generally have taken the train to Waddon, as I did. The journey from central London, via Balham, is easy, but it's a dull walk southwards down Purley Way towards the site.

The terminal itself ('Airport House') is set back from the main highway, and surrounded by side roads named for some of British aviation's most significant pioneers: Hawker Road and Imperial Way commemorate, respectively, the firm that built the Hurricane fighter plane, and the major pre-World War II airline that operated out of Croydon; there are many other 'tribute' roads nearby. Airport House has been a listed building since 1978; it's now a business centre, and also features a museum dedicated to the aerodrome. A four-engine de Havilland Heron passenger plane, mounted on struts above the path outside, is similar to the one that provided Croydon's final passenger flight (a departure to Rotterdam) in September 1959.

The building has been elegantly preserved, and it looked especially fine on the dazzlingly sunny day we photographed it. But its exterior, though undoubtedly striking, was a little too pristine for me. While time and decay have taken their toll on this book's other 'left behind' places, Airport House's immaculate façade lacks any signs of real-life wear and tear, and I missed the grimy manifestations of everyday operation that are so clearly and fascinatingly present in old photos of it.

A little further down the road, the area where aircraft took off and landed is covered in grass, as it always was; Croydon never had paved runways, and their absence was yet another reason for the airport's unsuitability for larger, heavier post-war passenger planes. On the field is a patch of concrete – possibly part of a taxi-ing route: a wide section (containing a white circle) points northwest, and a narrowing sliver leads north. We were momentarily puzzled to find temporary fencing around some of this: it had been erected by a group of model aircraft enthusiasts, for whom the spot is ideal for flying their planes. The wasp-like buzzing of the little engines contrasted with the deeper, softer rumble of traffic from the A23 – and with the occasional, more distant sounds of the jumbo jets far above us; but none of these noises disturbed the peace of the old airfield.

Because of its emptiness, it was easy to populate it with imaginings; and had we been here in the evening, the stories I'd read of ghostly air crash victims (such as the Dutch pilot who warns people about the fog that caused his plane to crash on take-off in 1936) would have been all the more credible.[177] In fading light and failing visibility, the "flat lonely spaces" of airfields have what David Beaty, a novelist who'd been a military and civilian pilot, described in *The Proving Flight* (1956) as "an essential sadness";[178] and even in brilliant sunshine, Croydon Airport's open spaces share it. But they also possess an almost tangible serenity – and on the day we visited, the stark solemnity of the War Memorial on the northeastern edge of the field (a "bronze eagle resting on an obelisk and a base of three square steps"[179]) was poignantly softened by the flowers it had just been decorated with.

Airport House flies a Union Jack; the Heron stands on the path in front of the building

On the airfield: this surviving area of concrete is an ideal place to fly model aircraft

The War Memorial, newly decorated with flowers, on the edge of the airfield beside the A23

Into the woods…the line beyond Chessington South that would have continued to Leatherhead. This photo was taken from the road bridge over the tracks

THE LINE TO CHESSINGTON

The concept of a 'five-year plan' quickly gained currency in the international political lexicon after Josef Stalin introduced the first one in 1928, so British newspaper readers wouldn't have been unduly surprised to see the term applied, seven years later,[180] to a report about a £30 million UK government programme of railway "reconstruction and improvement." The scheme had followed "months of negotiation" with the rail companies, and was intended to extend electrification and colour light signalling, produce more locomotives and rolling stock – and provide a seven-mile addition to the Southern Railway network in Surrey. This would head southwest beyond Motspur Park, via new stations at Malden Manor, Tolworth, Chessington Court, Chessington Grange and Malden Rushett, to a terminus at Leatherhead, giving that town a second route to London that would complement its existing one through Epsom.

By the summer of 1938, the new tracks had reached Tolworth; trains began to use the first section of line on May 28th, and as work continued towards Chessington, alterations were announced to the names of the two stations being built there: 'Court' would become 'North', while 'Grange' was to be 'South.'[181] Maybe a little razzmatazz was felt necessary to try and counteract the dullness radiated by these changes; for whatever reason, it was decided to promote the inauguration of this second stretch of metals by bringing in a local celebrity: Comet, a baby elephant from nearby Chessington Zoo. The animal had already appeared as a 'waiter' at the Trocadero Restaurant in London's Piccadilly,[182] and had been photographed trying to board a London bus earlier in the year;[183] but his participation in the opening ceremony at Chessington South, carried out by Surbiton's Deputy Mayor on 26th May 1939, proved to be a mixed blessing. According to the *Daily Herald*, "Comet failed to appreciate the dignity of his position. He soon got tired of the proceedings and sought diversion by chasing the builder's workmen off the premises."[184]

The line to Malden Rushett and Leatherhead was never completed – initially due to wartime restrictions, and subsequently because of Green Belt legislation. However, rails were laid for a short distance beyond Chessington South (39 chains – just under half a mile – according to the *Track Atlas of Mainland Britain*[185]), and 1950s maps indicate that there was a coal yard beside them; this later developed into a coal concentration depot,[186] and remained in place until 1988.

The area immediately to the west, between the coal yard tracks and Leatherhead Road (A243), has a more surprising history. In the spring of 1943, a substantial part of the Ordnance Survey map making operation – whose base in Southampton had been badly damaged by Nazi bombs on 30th November and 1st December 1940 – moved into "a large specially built hutted site"[187] here; its buildings had been hurriedly constructed the previous winter.[188] These makeshift premises, originally intended as temporary, served as the cartographers' headquarters until 1966, and some OS staff were still occupying them in the early 1970s. The huts, of course, are long gone; the Barwell Business Park has been erected over the area where they stood. And the Zoo that was home to Comet the elephant – among its other attractions were a "delightful Circus Aquarium and Pets Corner"[189] - has since become a fully fledged theme park, Chessington World of Adventures: it lies a little south of the Business Park, on the opposite side of the road.

***

Chessington South station, like the others on this line, was designed (or, at least, inspired) by the Southern Railway's Chief Architect, James Robb Scott (1882-1965).[190] Although only one of its two concrete-canopied platforms is in use, both have electrified tracks beside them. South of the platforms, these lines continue into the woods, where they come to an end; a good view of them can be had from the Garrison Lane railway bridge, outside the station.

What's visible on the bridge and in our photos reminds me of the classic *Start-rite* children's shoe advertisements, in which two kids are pictured "walking happily ever after" down a tree-lined path that recedes into an infinite distance. But Chessington's trees are far more sprawling than those in the *Start-rite* artwork (I haven't been able to confirm the story that World of Adventures staff cut down and feed the branches to their livestock), and the trackbed is rough and untidy – no place for trespassers of any sort, let alone children with neatly buckled sandals. And though, even at their vanishing point, the *Start-rite* trees seem to stay distinct from the road between them, the spot where the Chessington South lines are engulfed by their surroundings is still just about within range of our eyes and lenses...leaving us straining to penetrate the leafy curtain that has closed, tantalisingly, across it.

Is there another way into the woods? No access was possible via the Business Centre, but Chalky Lane, further down Leatherhead Road, seemed, initially, more promising: it runs east-to-west, beyond the southern limit of the old tracks, and might have provided a 'back door route' through the trees. But sadly, there was no such path; and, in any case, what could we have expected it to lead to? No more, perhaps, than sleeper fragments and discarded shards of metal like those we'd often seen beside other railway lines. So once I'd accepted the fruitlessness of any physical search, I was left with conjecture, fantasy – and the memory of a poem by

Rudyard Kipling that put things into a different perspective:

> They shut the road through the woods
> Seventy years ago.
> Weather and rain have undone it again,
> And now you would never know
> There was once a road through the woods
> Before they planted the trees.
> It is under the coppice and heath
> And the thin anemones...[191]

Ultimately, not even the 'permanent way' can withstand the erosions of time and nature; and although, as recently as 2001, there was a Parliamentary question about "the advantages of extending southwards the railway line from Chessington South,"[192] nothing now seems likely ever to halt the encroachment of the trees and undergrowth here.

At Chessington North: the station's platforms, with their distinctive canopies; and a view of the route southwards, showing a group of gangers walking towards the station, while a train from Chessington South approaches behind them

Chessington South lies just over half a mile beyond Chessington North, and its platform canopies share the same design. However, only the platform on the right in the photo below is in use

Beside the Thames at Deptford

DEPTFORD TO 'THE JAWS OF THE OCEAN' AND RED SANDS

The Thames, when I lived in Central London, never seemed to me like an Old Father, or even much like a working river. My occasional glimpses of it suggested, instead, something more supple and feminine; a model or a dancer, basking and preening on a catwalk course between her bridges, with a shining surface that creased, tightened and relaxed in the sun or moonlight like a film of flimsy silk.

From my present, more easterly home, the scene is different, as is the river itself. Downstream from Limehouse, the Thames develops into a harsher, more masculine and sinewy waterway that can pose considerable hazards to its shipping – though it no longer seems prone to conditions like the "dreadful storm of wind and rain" (referred to in a headline as a "tremendous hurricane") that battered the metropolis on New Year's Eve in 1833. On that day, ships "broke from their moorings...[and] people on the decks and seats of the barges, lighters and wherries were compelled to throw themselves on the bottoms of their vessels, to save themselves from being blown into the river."[193] Even in less extreme weather, the Thames, during its heyday as a route for waterborne traffic, was a place where collisions were frequent, and even shipwrecks not unknown. The stretch of water around Greenwich and Deptford (whose name derives from the long-since bridged 'deep ford' at the mouth of the River Ravensbourne) is often mentioned in accounts of mishaps. In 1737, "the Wind, blowing very fresh when the Tide turn'd, occasioned the Water to be very rough, by which two Boats from Greenwich were unhappily lost; one between Deptford and London...and another at the Isle of Dogs":[194] a total of fifteen people were drowned. And in 1817, "some bad management" of a small pleasure boat in "a sudden gust of wind" led to three young men being "immersed in the water" off Deptford;[195] two were rescued, but one died.

Larger craft, too, had their share of disasters: in January 1880, "the screw collier *Cleanthes*...from Newcastle, coal laden", was lying at anchor when she was struck at Bugsby's Reach, off the Greenwich Peninsula, by a cargo ship heading home to Liverpool. There were no casualties, but the *Cleanthes* "sunk abreast of the petroleum moorings in mid-channel."[196] Colliers were workhorse vessels, lacking the glamour of the "East Indiamen, brigs, brigatines...frigates [and] sloops-of-war" that could also be seen on the Victorian Thames;[197] but the capital had an insatiable need for their coal, shipped, mostly from Tyneside, for little more than ten shillings (50p) per ton.[198]

One of the colliers' hungriest customers was the London Electric Supply Corporation, whose huge Central Station, built near Creek Street (now Creek Road) in Deptford, opened in 1889. It occupied "a 3-acre site called The Stowage, which had once housed the store rooms, rigging sheds, mast sheds and sail lofts of the East India Company";[199] and its massive generators, driven by coal-fired steam, were designed to provide power for up to two million electric lights. Deptford was an ideal place for such a plant: land was cheap, and the river would not only facilitate the delivery of "sea-borne supplies of coal", but also provide abundant quantities of the water necessary for both steam-raising and cooling.[200]

The "Michelangelo of [the Deptford] installation," as the *Electrical Engineer* described him in October 1888,[201] was Sebastian de Ferranti, the London Electric Supply Corporation's 'Engineer and Electrician.' Still in his twenties, he planned and supervised almost every detail of its development, but changes and restrictions were imposed on his schemes after an intervention by the Board of Trade, and a fire at the new power station in November 1890 was followed by other setbacks. Ferranti lost the confidence of his directors, became disillusioned, and left the company in August 1891. Ironically, his Deptford plant was to prove highly successful; and under the auspices of LESCo's successor, the London Power Company, a new station, Deptford West, opened alongside it in 1929. Ferranti's original facility was "rejuvenated"[202] in the 1950s by the British Electricity Authority, the nationalised body that had taken over UK electricity generation after World War II; however, the entire Deptford site closed in 1983, and its buildings had been demolished by 1992. All that now remains of it is a landing stage – the jetty, over 100 yards long, where colliers (of which the London Power Company had its own fleet) used to moor while unloading.

***

Though the power station's jetty is visible from the Thames path that can be reached by turning off Creek Road towards Waitrose and Costa, and continuing northwest over a footbridge across the mouth of Deptford Creek, it's best seen from the shore at low tide. To get down to river level, take the stairs at the end of Watergate Street. The views from here are striking, but your legs and feet will pay a toll for exploring them. The curious, initially pleasing sensation of walking along the sloping shingle soon becomes a struggle; every step risks a slip, and alongside you is a partially soaked band of mud and weeds that the lapping tide, when it turns, will encroach upon with startling swiftness. But from the pathway above, the landing stage won't loom over you as impressively as it does down here; nor will you fully appreciate the throaty power of passing boats' engines. And this close to the water, it becomes apparent that you're a 'stranger on the shore' – an intruder upon the rhythms of the river that are gradually, concurrently with rust and rain, bringing ruin to what's already been labelled a 'dangerous structure.'

Perhaps someone will step in to save the old jetty. In 2010, it was sold to a property developer for just £1, plus maintenance costs and Port of London Authority licensing fees,[203] but little seems to have been done to it since then, and its most numerous and contented users are the seabirds that congregate on its railings and timbers. Uncertainty also surrounds Twinkle Park, which lies a few yards inland, bordered by Watergate Street and Borthwick Street. Named for a Mrs. Twinkle who once supervised a nearby recreation ground, it was conceived as a conservation and play area, and, when it opened in 1999, boasted a number of impressive features, including a pond and a space for floodlit ball games.[204] The pond seems to have drained away, though a couple of the other attractions, a gazebo and a little metal play-boat, are still in place, and the spot exudes a melancholy charm.

***

It's tempting to feel disappointed by the apparent failure of Twinkle Park to establish itself, and by the crumbling state of the jetty. But neglect and eventual ruin − or swifter removal by demolition - is the common fate of everything unwanted in London, and the indignant question posed by the graffito on a faded 'local heritage' sign at the end of Wharf Street, parallel to Watergate Street - "THIS IS HISTORY WHERE HAS IT GONE?" - can be answered with a shrug: after all, physical aspects of our past are perpetually crumbling and vanishing all around us. The feelings they inspire, even as they do so, have been set out in Rose Macaulay's *Pleasure of Ruins* as "admiration for the ruin as it was in its prime...aesthetic pleasure in its present appearance...association[s], historical or literary...and a dozen other entwined threads of pleasurable and melancholy emotion."[205] I'd suggest an additional category: the odd sensation we experience in the presence of something poised, as if on a tightrope, between survival and disintegration. 'Can it stay in place?' we may wonder, gazing at a vulnerable edifice. Will the 'cavalry' (in the form of cash injections or renovations) come riding over the horizon to save it? Or is any attempt at preservation doomed, and are we witnessing its final days? Questions like these have often arisen in relation to some of the abandoned places we've visited, but seem especially relevant to the very last of them: the Red Sands Maunsell Fort in the Thames Estuary.

Guy Maunsell, the civil engineer who designed and built this and other coastal defences during World War II, had constant battles with sceptical officialdom. After one bruising meeting at the Admiralty, he's reported to have "risen from the table" and delivered an angry parting shot to those still sitting around it: "Gentlemen, as you know, I live on a dairy farm at Hildenborough in Kent. When I leave the office, I go home and the first thing I do is go into the field where my cows are and discuss my day with them. I must say, I get more bloody sense from them than I ever get from talking to you!"[206] But once adopted, his often unconventional ideas almost invariably proved practical and cost-effective.

His sea forts – created in response to the dropping of mines in the Thames Estuary, and enemy air attacks on London and Liverpool - were constructed on dry land, and towed out to their offshore locations. There were two types: first to appear were four 'Naval' forts, intended to attack mine-laying planes: each had a submerged base supporting a pair of concrete pillars, and was topped off with a platform for anti-aircraft guns, to form what's been described as "a manned triumphal arch."[207] Placed off the East coast in 1942, they had crews of about 120 men, who lived inside the pillars. Mine-laying missions were already regarded by the Luftwaffe as especially hazardous – their pilots "came to loathe [them] since [they] required aircraft to fly low and slow"[208] - and the Naval forts were able to reduce their effectiveness and safeguard shipping.

The first of Maunsell's 'Army' forts was erected in Liverpool Bay in October 1942; two more were installed there, and three in the Thames Estuary. They were located closer to the shore than their Naval counterparts, and their design was different: each fort comprised seven walkway-connected 'houses' (one for observation, another with a searchlight, and five more with guns) supported on four legs, and rising to a height of 117 feet above the sea. 265 men were stationed on a fort for six weeks at a time.

The forts protecting the Mersey "never fired a shot in anger,"[209] and none of them survives. The Thames Estuary forts brought down 22 enemy planes and 30 flying bombs, but their post-war history has been a sorry tale of redundancy, decommissioning by the armed forces in the 1950s, and – in some cases – destruction as the result of demolition, weather damage or collisions. They have also been sporadically occupied by pirate radio station operators - while the former HM Fort Roughs, the most northerly of the Naval forts, was declared to be the 'Independent Principality of Sealand' in 1967. The only complete, seven-tower Maunsell Army fort is now Red Sands; it dates from 1943, and is reachable by a six-mile sea journey from the little town of Queenborough on the Isle of Sheppey.

***

Boat trips to Red Sands are comparatively easy to arrange, but accessing the fort itself is more complicated, and we were able to obtain permission to climb onto it and photograph it thanks to the kind cooperation of Project Redsand, the charity that's seeking to "restore...maintain and develop" the structure, and to make it available for events such as "weddings and corporate outings." Their more ambitious plans have included the development of "recording studios...a wartime and broadcasting museum", and even a luxury hotel on the fort.[210]

After walking up from Queenborough railway station to the town's ATL ('all tide landing') jetty, we boarded the *X-Pilot* ('Kent's Classic Pilot Vessel') for our sea journey eastwards. As we cast off, and I looked around, it was easy to appreciate this area's strategic wartime importance. Soon, I could see Southend and the mouth of the Thames (shrouded, that day, in fierce storm clouds) over to port; and I strove to shut out the wind and the *X-Pilot's* throbbing engine by calling to mind long-gone voices associated with it: the old songs of the collier crews bringing their vital cargoes down the east coast and up-river to Deptford...

> May Wear, and Tyne, and Thames ne'er freeze,
> Our ships and keels will pass with ease,
> Then Newcastle, Sunderland, and Shields
> Will still uphold the Coal Trade...[211]

...the ferocious words of the Luftwaffe pilots, who, after crossing the sea, used the Thames as a guide towards London, which they sought to destroy with their bombs and guns...

...The 'sharks' are [overhead] again. Protected by their fighters, German bombing planes can carry out their attacks unhindered. 7,000 metres are [now] between the German airplanes and the burning capital of a dying empire, 7,000 metres obscured by rising flames and choking smoke. Still, the path of the Thames is clear through the haze. A fresh wind from the west blows the smoke to the side for a moment, and the German He-111s fly through, their bomb bays releasing their payloads...[212]

...and the dry, scholarly tones of Guy Maunsell, informing the Admiralty of the successful installation of his Shivering Sands Army fort (a little to the east of Red Sands), whose presence would help prevent future airborne attacks...

...The final floating out operation sailed...on December 13 [1943], whereafter it transpired that the last of the Towers was grounded on the Shivering Sand in bright moonlight and bitter cold shortly after midnight on December 14...All the work in question was founded on the original conception of building individual units complete with all their equipment before leaving port so that they might then like Minerva emerge fully armed from the head of Mars...[213]

I was brought back from my reverie by the realisation that we were almost level with the fort. I'd seen it in photographs, watched a 1940s archive film of it in use,[214] and read numerous descriptions likening its towers to something out of a science-fiction movie. Its alien quality is undeniable, but my overwhelming first impression was of its menace: those brutal-looking 'houses', with their railings and fortifications, would have struck terror into passing enemy aircraft pilots – and were undoubtedly intended to. Perhaps my own unease was fuelled by the prospect of the vertiginous ladder climb I'd be facing when we docked. In fact, I managed the first part of it fairly easily, though I had to seek advice from our Project Redsand host about how best to swing off the rungs and onto the first platform of the tower we were boarding.

Once inside, we knew that our time on the fort would be limited, and began a hurried exploration of the 'house's' two stories and the open surface above them. Dirt and rust were all around. In Red Sands' active days, I'm sure everything would have been spotlessly clean, but decades of salty damp have had their effect, and despite the presence of a stove, radiators, a spectacularly filthy bath, supplies of toilet paper, and other essentials (even an elderly computer!), anyone spending the night here would be in for an uncomfortable time. Little military atmosphere survived, and conditions resembled those of a squat, or the kind of grubby 'dens' created in abandoned huts and caves by small boys – myself included – as little refuges from the comforts of home: spaces to call one's own, and to play and revel in for a few hours until night starts to fall and the temperature drops.

Climbing onto the top of the 'house' afforded us a bleak view of the surrounding sea; a nearby buoy tolled in the wind, and the flaky supports and uneven concrete deck were depressingly decrepit. To my surprise, we were able to capture on film just about everything that attracted our attention during our brief time on Red Sands, and I had few regrets as we prepared to leave it, and make our cautious descent back to the boat.

On our return voyage to Queenborough, I gazed back at the fort as it receded, and reflected on its now visibly failing powers of endurance. I'm glad it's still standing, but I'm less sure what it stands *for*...and it's clear that without serious help, its days are numbered. Of the various suggested renovation schemes, the plan to establish a museum on the site may have the most potential – especially if, at the same time, Red Sands can be restored and preserved as a permanent memorial to the Maunsell Forts, their creator, and the brave personnel who manned them and helped to protect London by doing so. I find it harder to imagine a high-end hotel with a helicopter pad out there, and fear that it would obliterate any recognisable trace of the 1940s fort that still casts its uneasy gaze over the Estuary.

The Thames: "a sinewy, masculine waterway" as it follows its course out of London

The power station's old jetty, seen from two angles on these pages:
first, looking towards Greenwich…

…and here, northwest along the shoreline

Above: In Twinkle Park
Below: A man-made water feature beside the shore near Deptford's Watergate Street

En route to Red Sands: Queenborough station; and (below) the water's edge. The town's All Tide Landing is a little further up the coastline

Red Sands from a distance - and closer-to

"These brutal-looking 'houses', with their railings and fortifications, would have struck terror into approaching enemy aircraft pilots…"

Studies in corrosion…outside and inside a Red Sands 'house'

POSTSCRIPT

One of the factors uniting all the 'abandoned places' in this book is the sometimes struggling stand they've made against the 'change and decay' of modern life – and, more broadly, against time itself. The dismissive phrase, "You're history!" implies indifference and disregard; but the sites we've featured will be part of London's 'here and now' for as long as they remain intact and visible. Ultimately, their 'histories' (the information and stories that can be gathered and told about them) may be secondary to the simple facts of their survival, their striking appearance, and their continued impact upon us. And it seems fitting that the Thames should flow so prominently though these final pages, playing its always ambiguous role – as provider, destroyer, input and output - in relation to our capital.

NOTES

INNER ZONE
BISHOPSGATE'S BRICK SPINE

[1] *Bell's New Weekly Messenger*, 5/7/1840
[2] *British Transport Historical Records – Eastern Counties*, quoted in *British History Online: Bishopsgate Railway Terminus*
[3] *Morning Advertiser*, 3/11/1840
[4] Ibid.
[5] *Ipswich Journal*, 20/8/1881
[6] Ibid.
[7] *The Builder*, November 1843
[8] *Bell's New Weekly Messenger*, 5/7/1840
[9] *Ipswich Journal*, 20/8/1881
[10] *Broadgate Tower, City of London by SOM* (article by Rowan Moore), *The Architects' Journal*, 19/3/2009
[11] Ibid.
[12] See *Ancient Arches* (article by Sarah Wise), *Time Out*, 24/10/2006
[13] *The Goodsyard: embracing change, celebrating London* (design and access statement 465517)

THE CITY'S UNBUILT RAIL ROUTE

[14] George and Weedon Grossmith, *The Diary of a Nobody*. It first appeared in *Punch*, and was published as a book in 1892.
[15] Harry Mount, *Finding Pooter's House, The Spectator*, 8/10/2008
[16] *Dundee Courier*, 6/6/1898
[17] *St. James's Gazette*, 16/8/1904
[18] Ibid.
[19] *London Daily News*, 11/3/1907
[20] *Lancashire Evening Post*, 22/10/1903
[21] *Aberdeen Press and Journal*, 15/8/1906
[22] *Framlingham Weekly News*, 6/9/1913
[23] Department of the Environment *Report on the Accident that occurred on 28th February 1975 at Moorgate Station*, HMSO
[24] Ibid.
[25] Ibid.
[26] Ibid.
[27] *Route Factsheet 1, Great Northern inner suburban services*
[28] *The Diary of a Nobody*, Chapter 1
[29] Luigi Russolo, *The Art of Noises* (1913), quoted in Umbro Apollonio, *Futurist Manifestos* (1973), p.75

GOODMAN'S FIELDS VIADUCT AND 'THE TILBURY'

[30] *The Literary World*, 11/7/1840
[31] *London Daily News*, 24/6/1886
[32] Ed Glinert, *East End Chronicles* (2005), Chapter 12, *Blitz and Bombs*
[33] Ibid.
[34] *Celebrating Moore: Works from the Collection of the Henry Moore Foundation* (1998), p.187
[35] Richie Calder, *Carry On London* (1941), pp.38-9
[36] Quoted in Gavin Weightman & Steve Humphries, *The Making of Modern London* (2007), p.260

37   See Geoffrey Field, *Nights Underground in Darkest London* (2007), Cercles 17, p.188
38   *Daily Mirror*, 12/12/1941
39   Quoted in John R. Kellett, *The Impact of Railways on Victorian Cities* (2006), p.345
40   See *Eco-Thames Co-op/Pinchin Street Heritage Survey*

121 WESTMINSTER BRIDGE ROAD: 'THE SALLY PORT TO ETERNITY'

41   *Evening Standard*, 29/11/1849
42   Quoted in John M. Clarke, *The Brookwood Necropolis Railway* (third edition, 1995), pp.2-3
43   *Surrey Comet*, 11/11/1854
44   Ibid.
45   *Punch*, 17/9/1859
46   *London Daily News*, 9/4/1902
47   'Tenebratio' is Latin for 'darkening' or 'obscuration'.
48   Charles Dickens, *Martin Chuzzlewit* (1843-4), Chapter 19
49   Quotation from LNC's publicity.
50   According to the London Association of Funeral Directors, the first motorised hearse appeared in about 1906; other sources give a slightly later date.
51   Project Canterbury, *Arthur Henry Stanton* (anglicanhistory.org) – reproduced from Catholic Literature Association article, 1933. See also *Shoreditch Observer*, 5/4/1913.
52   Clarke, op.cit., p.23

MIDDLE ZONE
THE LIMEHOUSE CURVE

53   See *Morning Post*, 14/2/1878
54   Rudyard Kipling, *Big Steamers*, first published in *A School History of England* (Oxford, 1911)
55   See Brian Edwards, *London Docklands: Urban Design in an Age of Deregulation* (1992), p.173
56   Hugo Marchant, *Limehouse Basin: Description, Walking Routes and History* http://www.imvisitinglondon.com/limehousebasin.html
57   *Dockside Noises*, from Thomas Burke, *Song Book of Quong Lee of Limehouse* (1920)
58   Tim R. Smith, *The Limehouse Basin Accumulator Tower*, in *London's Industrial Archaeology No. 11* (Greater London Industrial Archaeology Society, 2013: http://www.glias.org.uk/journals/11-d.html)
59   Ibid.
60   See http://www.openhouselondon.org.uk/london/search/factsheet.asp?ftloh_id=2667
61   *Reynolds's Newspaper*, 21/1/1883
62   Joseph Conrad, *The Mirror of the Sea* (1906), 'In Captivity', Chapter XXXIII

PEDESTRIANS IN THE ROTHERHITHE TUNNEL

63   *Some Account of the Archway or Tunnel intended to be made under the River Thames*, in *The Repertory of Arts, Manufactures, and Agriculture, consisting of original communications, specifications of patent inventions, practical and interesting papers* (etc.) Volume VII, second series, 1816, p.373
64   Ibid.
65   *London Daily News*, 8/5/1906
66   *London Daily News*, 28/9/1906
67   See *London Daily News*, 7/4/1908
68   Ibid.
69   *London Daily News*, 2/3/1908
70   Various figures are stated; signs currently inside the tunnel give its length as 4,866 feet.

[71] E.H. Tabor, *The Rotherhithe Tunnel*, in *Engineering Wonders of the World*, ed. Archibald Williams (1909)

[72] *London Daily News*, 24/9/1908

[73] *Daily Herald*, 6/1/1914

[74] Tabor, op.cit.

[75] *Aberdeen Press and Journal*, 2/7/1913

[76] *Dundee Evening Telegraph*, 19/5/1926

[77] Ibid. See also *Dundee Evening Telegraph*, 2/7/1926

[78] The phrase comes from Matt Houlbrook, and is quoted in the online blog *Haunting Shadwell Stair* (hauntingshadwellstair.wordpress.com)

[79] *Exeter and Plymouth Gazette*, 14/12/1934

[80] *Gloucestershire Echo*, 10/1/1934

[81] *Report of the Medical Officer of Health for London County Council*, 1930

[82] *Derby Daily Telegraph*, 16/3/1931

[83] Quotes here are all from Iain Sinclair, *Downriver* (1991), *II: Riverside Opportunities, IX.*

MILLWALL: 'DESOLATION-LAND'

[84] William Camden, *Britannia: Midlesex* (sic), paragraph 28. Translated from the original Latin by Philemon Holland, 1610

[85] See *Isle of Dogs – Past Life, Past Lives* (https://islandhistory.wordpress.com/2014/09/07/the-walls/)

[86] British History Online – *The Isle of Dogs: Introduction* (www.british-history.ac.uk/survey-london/vols43-4/pp375-387); originally published by London County Council, 1994

[87] www.historic-uk.com/HistoryMagazine/DestinationsUK/Millwall/

[88] Thomas Wright, *Some Habits and Customs of the Working Classes* (1867), quoted on the *Victorian London* website (www.victorianlondon.org)

[89] *Household Words*, Vol. VII (21/5/1853), p.273

[90] George R. Sims, *Off the track in London*, *Strand* magazine, July 1905

[91] *Reynolds's Newspaper*, 2/10/1887

[92] Story and quotations from *Morning Post*, 27/12/1889 and *Lloyd's Weekly Newspaper*, 29/12/1889

[93] See *Millwall Park Management Plan, 2008 to 2018*, p.7 (London Borough of Tower Hamlets, January 2008)

[94] See John Christopher, *The London & Blackwall Railway – Docklands' First Railway* (2013), p.63

[95] *Isle of Dogs – Past Life, Past Lives* (https://islandhistory.wordpress.com/2015/08/10/millwall-park/)

[96] *Greater London Industrial Archaeology Society Notes and News - August 1986* (http://www.glias.org.uk/news/105news.html)

[97] *Evening News*, 11/3/1987

[98] J.P. Martin, *Uncle* (1964), p.9

A VIEW FROM THE EGGS BRIDGE

[99] The words form part of the subtitle of Raymond Bunker's *Built Environment Vol. 34, No.3, The State of Australian Cities* (2008)

[100] All these terms appear in planning proposals for Docklands seen by the author.

[101] Information from http://edithsstreets.blogspot.co.uk/

[102] Peter Thorsheim, *Inventing Pollution: Coal, Smoke and Culture in Britain since 1800* (2006), p.142

[103] *New Scientist*, 3/12/1994 (*Gummer buries list of poisoned land* by Fred Pearce)

[104] London Docklands Development Corporation press release (*Docklands linked to the National Motorway Network*), 29/9/1989

[105] From summary of paper on *The Limehouse Link Tunnel* - p.57 of *Green Development: Literature Search* (1996), available online at http://nepis.epa.gov

[106] Wikipedia defines 'grade separation' as "a method of aligning a junction of two or more surface transport axes at different heights (grades) so that they will not disrupt the traffic flow on other transit routes when they cross each other."

[107] *London Gazette*, 1/2/1990, pp.1401-2

[108] Drawing and two photographs can be seen at http://www.rooneyarchitects.com/lddc

[109] LDDC press release, 29/9/1989 (op. cit.)

[110] See 'Forbidden Road' postings on http://www.sabre-roads.org.uk, April 2011

[111] See http://www.filmoffice.co.uk

[112] TfL leaflet, *Have your say on the new Thames River Crossings*, October 2012, p.16

BESIDE THE TRACKS IN HAMMERSMITH AND EAST PUTNEY
[113] See http://www.getwestlondon.co.uk – article dated 14/10/2010

[114] *London Daily News*, 30/12/1868

[115] *London Evening Standard*, 30/12/1868

[116] *Morning Advertiser*, 25/12/1868

[117] Ibid.

[118] Christian Wolmar, *The Subterranean Railway* (2004), p.67

[119] Story and quotations from *Morning Advertiser*, 6/5/1869

[120] @danwaddell, tweeted on 11/5/2016

[121] For a clear map of this confusing section of track, showing present and past lines, see Joe Brown, *London Railway Atlas* (2006), pp.30-1

[122] Quotations from *Pall Mall Gazette*, 29/5/1889

[123] See post by James Dixon on http://www.putneysw15.com (16/02/2013)

[124] Joe Brown, op. cit., p.31

[125] See Journal of the London Underground Railway Society, issue no. 60 (Vol. 5 No. 12), December 1966, p.180

[126] See posts about 'Lifted flying junction, E. Putney-Clapham Jc', www.districtdavesforum.co.uk, October 2016

[127] See, for example, www.londonreconnections.com/2011/ellx-phase-two-clapham-junctions-platforms-1-and-2/

OUTER ZONE
AN INTERLUDE AT MILL HILL EAST
[128] Quotations from *Illustrated Times*, 26/10/1867

[129] *Hendon & Finchley Times*, 12/4/1940

[130] Approximate figures based on those in John Marius Wilson's *Imperial Gazetteer of England and Wales*, 1870-2

[131] Information from National Gas Archive

[132] *Hendon & Finchley Times*, 12/4/1940

[133] http://www.millbrookpark.com/news/military-history-of-barracks-inspires-new-taylor-wimpey-development

[134] See stories by Matt Watts, *Evening Standard*, 22/9/2014, and Antonia Molloy, *The Independent*, 22/9/2014

[135] http://www.disused-stations.org.uk/m/mill_hill_east/

M12 – THE MOTORWAY THAT NEVER WAS
136 Sonnet from *The Comic Annual* by Thomas Hood, 1832
137 From *1907* in *The Years* by Virginia Woolf, 1937
138 See *Jennings Coaches of Ashen (Fact File 5)*, p.18 (Essex Bus Enthusiasts Group, 2003)
139 *Essex Newsman*, 1/8/1950
140 Story and quotation from *The Sphere*, 9/2/1957
141 www.british-history.ac.uk/vch/essex/vol6/pp338-344
142 See Civil Service document *Proposed Construction of New and Improvement of Existing Trunk Roads; Proposed M.12 Motorway Economic Study* (1972) In National Archives, Kew
143 *M12 Motorway: Traffic Study and Economic Appraisal* by Brian Colquhoun & Partners, Consulting Engineers (1972) In National Archives, Kew
144 See the 'Pathetic Motorways' site (http://pathetic.org.uk/unbuilt/m12/), and http://www.liquisearch.com/a12_road_england/m12_motorway
145 See previous note.
146 http://thelostbyway.com/tag/river-roding   The 'Ballardian' comment relates to J.G. Ballard's novel *Concrete Island* (1974)
147 Michael Drayton, *Poly-Olbion Part 2* (1622), *The nineteenth Song*. A note beside the verses explains that "Many Townes that stand on this River, have her name as an addition: as *Aythorpe Roding, Leaden Roding*, with many other."
148 *Chelmsford Chronicle*, 12/10/1877
149 See *Epping Forest in Ancient British Times*, *Gardeners' Chronicle* article reprinted in *Chelmsford Chronicle*, 16/6/1882
150 Krista A., posting on https://www.yelp.co.uk/biz/roding-valley-park-redbridge, 25/7/2011
151 See *Gallions Reach* chapter

THE CRESCENT WOOD TUNNEL
152 *Morning Post*, 12/6/1854
153 https://www.architecture.com/Explore/Buildings/CrystalPalace.aspx
154 *London Daily News*, 24/6/1863
155 *London Evening Standard*, 27/8/1863
156 The station's opening date is often given as 1/8/1884, but the press report quoted below appears to confirm that it was actually 1/9.
157 *Morning Post*, 2/9/1884
158 *Morning Post*, 1/10/1889
159 *London Daily News*, 31/1/1906
160 *The Stage*, 3/12/1936
161 See https://londoncallingblog.net/2016/05/22/new-louis-masai-street-art-in-sydenham-woods/ This site includes photographs of the mural.

CROYDON AIRPORT
162 *Lancashire Evening Post*, 15/12/1919
163 See *Illustrated London News* article, *The Growth of Civilian Aviation*, 26/6/1920
164 Quotations from *Cambridge Daily News*, 24/9/1920
165 *Illustrated London News*, 23/10/1920
166 *Tamworth Herald*, 11/6/1921
167 *Hansard*, 12/7/1923
168 *Dundee Evening Telegraph*, 4/4/1921
169 *Dundee Evening Telegraph*, 3/8/1921
170 See Ian Anderson, *Croydon Airport* (*Institution of Civil Engineers Panel for Historical Engineering Works Newsletter* No. 149, March 2016)

[171] http://www.croydonairport.org.uk

[172] Quoted by Brett Holman in *Stop the Planes* (14/11/2011), http://airminded.org/2011/10/14/stop-the-planes

[173] *By Air to London* (*Daily Mail*), reprinted in *Gloucester Citizen*, 16/5/1946

[174] See Chris Beanland, *The history of Heathrow, Independent*, 1/3/2011

[175] *The Scotsman*, 5/5/1947

[176] *Hansard*, 20/4/1964

[177] See *Haunting Tales from Croydon Airport*, 30/10/2010, http://www.yourlocalguardian.co.uk/news/local/topstories/8477137.Haunting_tales_from_Croydon_Airport/

[178] David Beaty, *The Proving Flight* (1956), Chapter 2

[179] From the official description of Croydon Aerodrome Battle of Britain Memorial by the Imperial War Museums.

THE LINE TO CHESSINGTON

[180] The following quotations are from *Nottingham Evening Post*, 5/11/1935 ('Five-Year British Rail Plan'); the story was extensively reported in other papers.

[181] See *Surrey Advertiser*, 14/1/1939

[182] Getty Images has a photo of this, dated 30/12/1938.

[183] See 'An Elephant Never Forgets', *Chelmsford Chronicle*, 10/2/1939

[184] *Daily Herald*, 27/5/1939

[185] See *Track Atlas of Mainland Britain* (2009), p.111

[186] Dr. Richard Beeching's report, *The Reshaping of British Railways* (1963), explains that coal concentration depots are sites "to which coal can be moved by rail for final road distribution to small industrial and domestic consumers."

[187] C.W. Phillips, *Archaeology in the Ordnance Survey 1791-1965* (1980), p.44

[188] https://ourwiki.ordnancesurvey.co.uk/index.php/Special:SearchByProperty/Description/RNLI-20Charity-20Work

[189] Chessington Zoo poster, 1939

[190] See entry for James Robb Scott in *Dictionary of Scottish Architects* (http://www.scottisharchitects.org.uk/)

[191] Rudyard Kipling, *The Way Through the Woods*, from *Rewards and Fairies* (1910)

[192] *Hansard*, 16/7/2001

DEPTFORD TO 'THE JAWS OF THE OCEAN' AND RED SANDS

[193] *Morning Advertiser*, 1/1/1834

[194] *Derby Mercury*, 21/4/1737 (reprinted from *St. James's Evening-Post*); punctuation modernised.

[195] Story and quotations from *Hampshire Chronicle*, 21/4/1817

[196] *London Daily News*, 5/1/1880

[197] *Illustrated London News*, 10/7/1886

[198] See *Illustrated London News*, 29/3/1890

[199] Supplement to *Histelec News No.25*, December 2003: *Ferranti's Deptford Power Station* ('extracted extensively from a pamphlet published by the CEGB in 1986 entitled *Cradle of Power – The Story of Deptford Power Stations* and written by Rob Cochrane.')

[200] See S.A. Murray, *Bankside Power Station: Planning, Politics and Pollution* (University of Leicester Ph.D thesis, 2014), p.9, p.44

[201] Quoted in *Histelec News* supplement, op. cit.

[202] *Histelec News*, op. cit.

[203] See http://www.eastlondonlines.co.uk/2010/12/charity-plans-washed-away-by-sale-of-jetty-2/

[204] See http://www.london-footprints.co.uk/wkdeptfordgrn.htm

[205] Rose Macaulay, *Pleasure of Ruins* (1953), pp.xv-xvi

[206] Quoted in Nigel Watson and Frank Turner, *Maunsell: The Firm and its Founder* (2005), p.35

[207] *Fort Madness: Britain's Bizarre Sea Defense against the Germans*, Spiegel Online, 12/11/2010

[208] Robert Forczyk, *We March Against England: Operation Sea Lion 1940-41* (2016), p.161

[209] Information and quotation from http://www.project-redsand.com/history.htm

[210] See http://www.project-redsand.com/project.htm and http://www.kentonline.co.uk/herne-bay/news/sea-fort-hotel-plans-unveiled-37603/

[211] From *The Coal Trade*, in *Allan's Illustrated Edition of Tyneside Songs and Readings* (1891)

[212] *Fighters Battle over London* from *German Propaganda Archive*, Calvin College, Michigan, USA. Translated from an article in *Kleine Kriegshefte* ('Little Warheads') #8, 1940

[213] Quoted in Watson & Turner, op.cit., p.33

[214] The film can be seen at the Museum of Docklands, West India Dock Road, E14 4AL. A model of a Maunsell Army fort, made for the Port of London Authority in 1946, is also on display there.

ABOUT THE AUTHORS

Nick Freeth has written extensively about music, transport, and American subjects - and thinks that his fascination with lonely, semi-abandoned places may have arisen during a journey down the USA's Route 66. He's published two guides to the famous highway, and in 2014, he contributed an essay on 'Words and Music' to the *Poetry by Heart* resource co-founded by former Poet Laureate Sir Andrew Motion. Two years later, Nick 'ghosted' the autobiography of Sir Michael Caine's stuntman, Johnny Morris.

Olivia Landsberg has been a passionate photographer for more than 25 years. She specialises in images that transcend time and place, and her mission is to help people see things in a different light. Olivia's work has been exhibited in London, Durham and in the US. As a radio producer, she has made programmes on photography for BBC Radio 4, including *The Spoken Image* with photographer Eamonn McCabe.